Wars R' Us

Taking Action for Peace

By

Otis Carney

ISBN: 1-4033-2800-5 (Paperback)
ISBN: 1-4033-2799-8 (e-book)
ISBN: 1-4033-3480-3 (Hardcover)

This book is printed on acid free paper.

Library of Congress Control Number: 2002091829

Printed in the United States
Bloomington, IN

1stBooks - rev. 06/25/02

Books by Otis Carney

LOVE AT FIRST FLIGHT (with Charles Spalding)
WHEN THE BOUGH BREAKS
YESTERDAY'S HERO
GOOD FRIDAY 1963
THE PAPER BULLET
NEW LEASE ON LIFE
WELCOME BACK BILLY RAWLS

CHIHUAHUA 1916
THE FENCE JUMPER
EDDIE BULWER'S GROUND
THROW THE RASCALS OUT
FRONTIERS
ISLAND GIRL
HOG HEAVEN
VICTORY OF SURRENDER
APACHE TEARS

To my lucky seven
Grandchildren
Tess, Joe, Nora, Hannah, Ella, Will, Louise Elizabeth
For your brave new world

"Come on, you sonofbitches, do you want to live forever!"

U.S. Marine Sergeant Major, Belleau Wood, France, 1917

"Kill Japs, kill Japs, kill Japs!"

Admiral William F. Halsey, Solomon Islands, 1943

Mark Twain's War Prayer

"O Lord our God, help us to tear their soldiers to bloody shreds with our shells; help us to cover their smiling fields with the pale forms of their patriotic dead; help us to drown the thunder of the guns with the shrieks of their wounded, writhing in pain; help us lay waste their humble homes with a hurricane of fire; help us to wring the hearts of their unoffending widows with the unavailing grief...stain the snow with the blood of their wounded feet! We ask it, in the spirit of love, of Him Who is the Source of Love...and seek his aid with humble and contrite hearts. Amen.

(In fear of giving offense or of actual reprisals, Mark Twain's family refused to let him publish his War Prayer until after his death.)

GETTING REAL

I was late waking up that morning.

Lay there in bed, watching the rising sun flame over the granite fists of the Wind River Mountains in Wyoming. It's cold up here in September. Mist was rising off the black snake of the Green River. A few mallards squawked into flight to catch the first sunbeams. Out in the frosty yellow meadows beyond our ranch house, Angus cows, though already haired up for winter, had their backs humped, stretching their cold limbs. I could almost hear them sighing as their big five hundred pound calves butted at their teats to get a wake-up suck.

Nothing much changes in this world of mine. Where our house stands, the Shoshones or possibly Sioux had a sweat lodge God knows how many years ago. We've found their teepee rocks and stone scrapers, some of them buried under three feet of topsoil. That's a lot of water down the river. In the sweat lodge they'd cook out their aches and pains, sniff the burning sage in their prayers, then plunge into the icy Green below. On a point of willows jutting into the river, a pair of sleek fat beaver splatted their tails and plunged underwater into their lodge. They were ready for whatever came. They'd already cut a brownish plew of willows, floating beside their house for their winter feed. Beaver have probably been using that same point forever. Ideal habitat, everything they want here—until the world came in and attacked them.

In the early 1800's, mountain men came whooping down to the Green. They saw the brown gold in it, these wildest of Scotch-Irish Americans and some Frenchmen who'd already conquered the Appalachian frontier. Bearded, boozers, brawlers, they'd hire Indians to trap for them. There were five Indian nations hunting this country where I live. The Indians were mostly peaceful then, a ready labor pool, all astounded by these strange hair faces who seemed to have dropped in from the sky and could dole out bright trinkets and sticks that could kill far better than arrows. When an Indian delivered his trapper boss a stack of beaver pelts as tall as a rifle, the trapper would give him the rifle. Once a year, right on these shores of the Green, the mountain men would all rendezvous, bartering with eastern shysters for their pelts, racing their horses, swapping Indian squaws. One helluva roaring time. With their blood and guts, they made the Green into the lifeblood of the fur trade. Nobody cared about conservation then. There'd always be enough of everything in this wild paradise. In their frenzy to sell beaver hats to the dandies of England, France and Germany, they all but trapped the river out.

But then, almost overnight, fashions changed. Silk hats were now the rage. The mountain men were suddenly disemployed, had no place to go. They gave a "waaugh" roar like a grizzly bear, spat out their chaws and shouldered their 20 pound Hawken flintlocks. Sometimes with their Indian squaws shuffling beside them, but mostly alone, they set out over the mountains to the unknown that lay beyond. They'd gambled or traded away their horses at the various rendezvous, so they were down to using the shank's mare. They walked. Foot-burned the rocks and deserts one thousand, two thousand miles. They trudged on angry and brave, kept following the sundown further west. Blazed the first trails to Oregon, California, New Mexico, Arizona. Opened up the fearsome wilderness. They handed it to us in the festering wounds of arrowheads that had punctured them, made us a gift of the greasy skins of animals they'd killed to stay alive. They gave us the great and grand USA. Ours forever.

To this day.

Hell, I didn't know the day. They're all the same out here. Beaver survive, we survive. Never had it so good, as we used to say when we came back from our last triumphant war.

The phone was ringing September 11th. My nephew from town. Town? Lucky to count a thousand people there. The whole county is as big as the state of Connecticut and has 5000 people. The rest are cattle, horses and wild animals. "Turn on your TV!" he cries. "Somebody has just crashed an airliner into the World Trade Center in New York!"

I went upstairs to where my wife Teddy hides our TV. She rarely watches it. I snapped on the TV just in time to see the second jet roar into the second tower. Awful violence, I'm fascinated, stay glued to it.

Minneapolis, 1948: Teddy has just given birth to our first son. I'm driving home late from the hospital, icy road, squeal the brakes. Ahead of me, two cars have hurtled off the pavement. On their backs, wheels spinning, doors sprung open, bodies lying in the icy grass. I'm frozen, don't want to watch, but can't resist. Somebody is covering a dead girl with a blanket. All I can see is her hair. It's brown. Exact color of Teddy's! Leap out, get blood on my hands, try to help! But I remain paralyzed, watching.

Only now, snap off the damn TV, images still flaming in my eyes. The jet slamming the tower, billows of av gas exploding! Jesus God, this again!

Guam, 1944. I'm in an outdoor shower, naked as a baby, my partner pilot beside me, soaping up. Then a roar. Over us, not twenty feet above us, a crippled B-29. Two engines out on one wing, black props windmilling helplessly. With a thundering tearing it plunges in, yards

5

from us. Av gas explodes, and more. This 29 is loaded with firebombs that would have burned out some city in Japan. They're crackling, searing holes in the twisted metal. The other pilot and I, still naked, run toward it, shielding our faces from the terrible heat. I'm close enough to see a waist gunner kid in his blister screaming at us, burning alive. Then we have to run, escape. Too late.

September 11th, I drifted out into the quiet of the sagebrush. In a sea of lacy gray shrubs shriveling up for winter, I catch sight of the white rumps of an antelope doe and her bouncy twin fawns. It's fear in her startled brown eyes, but also a kind of trust that she can move on and take care of her fawns. They trot away, up into the forests of aspen, showering down golden leaves. Quiet here forever. Turn off the roar of that suffering world out there.

Maybe you went out, too, that day, went somewhere, anywhere, just to get away. But we can't. Get real now, I tell myself. Powerless, way off in the sagebrush, you're just one more of the millions of nobodies, crying out in pain: how did we ever get ourselves into this fix, and what could I or you or any of us do to help get us out of it?

Like the auto wreck on the road, when I drive up and see it, I'm an innocent bystander to the tragic horror. But if I don't leap out of my car and try to help, get blood on my hands, aren't I a guilty bystander, too? I could have done, and I didn't.

Isn't there any way that I can lift myself up out of powerlessness, maybe even lift others, too, so that we can all find our way again, back to the blessed land that we knew and treasured, before this awful day?

Drop it, I warned myself. Don't get involved. Why do you, almost 80, have to leap up onto the ramparts again and try to fight somebody else's war? Nobody elected you some mini-Atlas trying to fling the world off of everybody's shoulders. The majority of Americans live in tense, rushing cities. What does the next siren mean? Where are the police cars screaming off to? No wonder they're afraid now. But out in the Big Open, you can't relate to any of that, can't possibly know how those people feel. Just keep the TV off, keep wading your quiet river throwing flies at trout in the precious years you have left.

But even on a lonely ranch, neighbor cowboys come by, trailing their herds down from the mountains. They'll hook a leg on the saddle horn, take a pinch of Copenhagen and ask: whyinhell, why this goddamn thing? A bearded vet, shot seven times as a Navy Seal in Nam, spits it out. "Send us over there, we'll get every one of them dirty sonsofbitches." Young cousins come down to go fishing, but they don't have TV at their house. Can they look at mine? One of my granddaughters brings over her boyfriend. He's from Scotland, it's all new to him here. Grandpa, she asks, what the devil is going on? How bad is it going to get?

Nobody knows, surely not me. As Mother Theresa said, "Only a few of us are cut out to do great things." On the other hand, and maybe she was right: "all of us can do small things in a great way."

Well, the one small thing I do know, the one try I can make, is to write from my gut the sadness I feel. Let it out. For three days I hammer words on my computer,

then fax an op-ed piece to the <u>Casper Star Tribune</u>, which is pretty much the state paper of Wyoming. In the article I strongly opposed our rush to vengeful war.

Usually, you sail your paper airplane out there and never hear a word back. But now, E-mails, phone calls, letters. Even the paper's editor thanking me for saying what I had. My God, I thought, did I strike a nerve here. What is it?

Then I got a letter hand-written on copy book paper. "I've been working a shutdown at the power plant. Bought a Sunday paper, re-read it that night before bed. It was what God reputedly loves, The Truth! I made 10 photo-copies of it, mailed them to family members and loved ones. It has got to be one of the best essays in this and any other language. I took it to work, shared it with brother carpenters who 'heard you' loud and clear. If somebody retains the child-like courage to call a spade a shovel, as you have, then you will have become a veritable beacon to the rest of us. May God bless you, Mr. Carney. You remind me of the importance of suiting up and showing up every day and trying to use your head

for something besides a hat rack. Gratefully yours, Tom Burke."

I didn't realize it then but his words made me begin. There are perhaps millions of us out there like Tom Burke. We want to know the truth about this tragedy. Be patriotic citizens and do our best to keep it from happening again.

Is there anything I do know from my own experience that might help?

Nothing earth-shaking, Tom, but now that you've put me on the road, here's what I'd suggest:

GETTING REAL. Facing up to the fix we're in.

DIGGING OUT THE TRUTH. Learning what caused it.

RESISTING WAR PROPAGANDA: Spiking the lies that keep us from truth.

LIVING IN POSITIVE, NOT NEGATIVE EMOTIONS. Taking back our power with life-enhancing emotions rather than remaining powerless in death-enhancing ones.

TAKING POLITICAL ACTION. Stand up and be counted. Become active citizens committing ourselves to helping stop the violence.

Do our small thing, each of us, in the greatest way we know.

Thanks for the letter, Tom. Here's to getting real. You take the spade and I'll take the shovel. Maybe between us we can dig our way out of this fix.

GETTING REAL IS CARING ABOUT WHAT'S GOING ON IN THE WORLD

"The history of civilization has been repetitive horror which culminated in the last century with the slaughter and mayhem of millions of people.

"Yet still, there were always individuals of higher consciousness and spiritual advancement who protested the ways of destruction. Society soon labeled them as the enemy, unpatriotic, cowards who had to be silenced. To not go along with socially current delusions threatens power structures which are based on spiritual error. The rule of guilt, sin and fear is indeed threatened by a God of infinite mercy, compassion and unconditional love..."

David R. Hawkins, MD, Ph.D, author and pioneer in consciousness research.

*

I like to think of heaven, or peace, as the space and the blessed silence between thoughts.

I can even hope that the silence is a sacred space where one can hear one's heart, and surrender to its longing to feel and act out of unconditional love. Mercy. Compassion.

What a tremendous order!

How can any of us shut out the thoughts gabbling in our brains, the ceaseless roar of TV, the white noise of angry opinions and the needing to be "right" that our egos demand us to accept as being our meaning, the truth of our lives? How can we give up the illusion that our need to control, to win, to survive is the only real world? Has humanity come that far? Are we there yet?

I'm certainly not. But I truly want to be. To somehow get beyond the ego fantasies, rigidities and thoughts that are no more than arrogant projections out of a lower consciousness, and hence are basically worthless and only create more strife.

Sad to say, this book is filled with exactly such perceptions, mine and from others. But except for this positionality, this taking sides, I know no other way to dramatize what seems to me to be the danger and futility of our Wars R'Us mentality. Thus I've relied on respected voices to tell the truth as they see it. They're the experts in war and peace, which I can't pretend to be.

A logical question is: why listen to this guy? What does he know? Nothing, really, except what I've seen with my own eyes and experienced. At least, these things did happen to me and I drew conclusions from them, however flawed and ego edited. But it's the sum of them that led me to write this book.

I plead guilty that it's old fashioned, emotional, and has the trigger word, *spiritual*, at its root. Why? Because I'm convinced that it's in the human spirit where the war is being waged and where it will be decided. Depending on the degree of our mercy, compassion and unconditional love hangs the destiny of Americans and the world.

I love my country.

I'm convinced that there are specific ways that every patriot can come to its aid. I try to dramatize some of them. They are out there in a rising consciousness that speaks to a new kind of humanity, a new mind. As Einstein said: "No problem can be solved out of the same consciousness that caused it."

When you and I are threatened by a dreadful and never before experienced peril, our country needs you and me and every one of us. More than ever, we need each other if we hope to rise to the challenge facing us.

This book is about Hope. The hope that in our joining, our patriotic bonding, each of us, in our own unique and powerful ways, will activate our love of country. How? By standing up and being counted as responsible citizens, making our voices heard in our nation's governance.

We're still blessed with freedom and free speech, but they're only empty words unless we commit ourselves to using them to help shape the future of our beloved America.

And yes, when we see our government taking actions in our name, when we know in our heart that they seem unjust or harmful to ourselves and to humanity at large—then love of country must include constructive criticism, and counter-action, citizen action, to change any negative policies that threaten not only our cherished freedoms, but eventually, God forbid, our personal and national survival.

I've written many books about soldiers and the battles they have fought. I love our military men and women for their centuries of raw guts in defending our flag. They did it with honor for all of us, and they're still out there on the firing line, putting themselves in harm's way, even sacrificing their lives so that we may live ours in peace.

But how to preserve that peace, what method to use when we're under attack, seems to me a vital question that both the soldier and the patriot have a duty to ask.

Is traditional war the right response? Cruise missiles, smart bombs, depleted uranium bombs, armored divisions, high tech ground forces, and now even leaked and chilling scenarios about using nuclear weapons— madness, isn't it? Are these the only possible solution?

Or could it be that we are responding to an ancient human reflex that seeks to fight the wars of old in a world that used to be, but is not our world anymore? If this is true, then shouldn't we be searching for a new broader world-view, a new hope that here might lie the way to meet our present challenges without resorting to the last resort of war?

To ask that question is neither cowardice nor disloyalty, but rather a spiritual concern, a heart-felt caring for the sacredness of all life. In this broader, humanitarian vision, the patriot and his or her leaders believe deeply that the lives of Americans (or their enemies, for that matter) are too precious to be squandered in vain.

Why did terror strike us? What can we do about it now?

It seems to me there are two understandable reasons why we rushed into war to avenge the tragedy of 9/11. In military parlance it was "AOS", all options stink. In the natural public outcry over our massive wounding, it was also the desperate patriotic demand: SOMETHING HAS TO BE DONE!

This urgency led us to respond with the familiar and oldest reflex in the psyche of mankind. An Enemy from Out There approaches us in our cave, threatens us and finally attacks. What do we do? By primordial reflex, we can only strike back. It's kill or be killed.

Furthermore, the reflex of resorting to war, the joining together to fight a common enemy is history's oldest bonding mechanism. It has unified one tribe to fight another ever since we were still in the caves. The victors became nations and have governed since time immemorial by rallying their people again and again to fight the next war.

Now, by declaring war against the people of Afghanistan and named and unnamed terrorists and terrorist nations, we did indeed fire a resounding warning shot at the world. We put meaning into the banner on our old flag: Do Not Tread on Me.

All options stunk. Something had to be done. We did it.

But did we win? Have we won?

To Sir Michael Howard, Oxford and Yale professor of military history and strategist for the United Kingdom in the Cold War: "It is like trying to eradicate cancer cells with a blowtorch. Whatever its military justification, the bombing of Afghanistan, with the inevitable 'collateral damage' it causes, will gradually whittle away the immense moral ascendancy that we enjoyed as a result of the bombing of the World Trade Center. Every fresh picture on television of a hospital hit, or children crippled by land mines, or refugees driven from their homes by Western military action will strengthen the hatred of our adversaries, swell the ranks of the terrorists, and sow fresh doubts in the minds of our supporters.

"Could it have been avoided? Certainly, and rather than what President Bush so unfortunately termed 'a crusade against evil doers'—that is, a military campaign conducted by an alliance dominated by the United States—many people would have preferred a police operation conducted under the auspices of the United Nations on behalf of the international community as a whole, against a criminal conspiracy that should be hunted down and brought before an international court, where they would receive a fair trial and if found guilty, awarded an appropriate sentence. In an ideal world, that is no doubt what would have happened.

"But we do not live in an ideal world. The 'war' word has been used and cannot be withdrawn; and its use has brought inevitable and irresistible pressure to use military force as soon, and as decisively as possible."

Howard's conclusion: "Prolongation of the war is likely to be so disastrous. Even more disastrous would be its extension, as American opinion seems increasingly to demand, in a 'Long March' through other 'rogue states' beginning with Iraq, in order to eradicate terrorism for good, all so that the world can live at peace. I can think of no policy more likely not only to prolong the war indefinitely but to ensure that we can never win it."

Men like Sir Michael Howard are questioning and searching for a better way for all of us. The patriot has to mourn the centuries of wars our people have had to fight. Because, in some cases, history shows, those wars have proven unnecessary to the welfare of our nation. Was the genocide wreaked on the Seminole Indians a "war of national defense", as President Zachary Taylor called it at the time. Could a handful of aborigines have seriously threatened the Manifest Destiny of the United States?

Suppose they had just been left alone? Or, as Lincoln said about the Civil War, "Rich man's war, poor man's fight." Too often, for the interests of the few, the many have been sacrificed. That's the tragic part. To die for lost causes that never should have led to war.

Toward this end, I've tried to dramatize in brief, non-heroic personal experience not only "Why War?" but to question the alleged reasons for it, the fatal bugle calls that have rallied mankind for our entire existence. Rather than being swept away by lofty slogans manipulating our patriotism, the kill or be killed imperative, might we want to feel for a moment the emotional gut wrench, the dirt and stink and blood of what actual war really is?

I've also dramatized from my own experience the "selling of war," done with the best intentions by honorable, patriotic Americans. When a public is overwhelmed, as we are now, by war propaganda—and much of it being trumpeted by secure, comfortable civilians who have never heard a shot fired—I want them only to ask the men who have been there and been shot at. Listen to them, please, before you rush their sons and grandsons and now their daughters into the maw to do it again.

Do you or I or any of us really know where we are now? And where do we go from here?

None of us, certainly not me, have the whole truth. We only know 'about.' We don't *know*. We're not privy to

21

state secrets. As an old civilian, far out of the fray, I've never fought a terrorist in my life, wouldn't know where to start. But like you, we still have eyes and ears, gut instincts.

Let's use them. Take a hard look at what's happening and see if we like it this way. Or could we begin to "just say no," and to take the actions each of us feel are needed to get us to "yes." To get us possibly to another way beyond the roar of war, and someday, God willing, to have stacked the arms of anger and vengeance, and be marching instead on the longed-for road to peace.

Isn't it time for a moment to turn off the ceaseless rhetoric of war, the drum beat of war thoughts. Turn off their barrage on TV, let them go. And in the new quiet, listen to truth, listen to what our heart tells us inside, not simply what we are being told from outside.

I wrote this book because I saw and felt something coming that I believe is harmful to my country and eventually the world at large. When I see a war against a single terrorist broaden slowly into a war against worldwide groups of terrorists—and further still, in the alerts and fears that have been showered upon us, to broaden into an attack on our personal freedoms at home—and yet further to widen into expanding potential attacks on many identified nations, so called "Evil,"—at this point my Distant Early Warning System is triggered.

I have to ask myself, in my own life, and perhaps you in yours: Where have we heard this before? Haven't we been there and done that for too long? The reason why we've done it is what patriots must look at, expose, and change.

The America I knew and still love was a Republic. That's what we fought for. To preserve it.

But what have we been fighting for ever since the end of World War II? Isn't it a new kind of America, no longer a Republic, but now an economic Empire preserved and expanded by the use of our overwhelming military force? The mind-searing symbols of 9/11 were not chosen by accident. The crashing World Trade Center the dollar sign of the New World Order, and the flaming Pentagon, the near miss on our military heart.

Driven by these symbols, I believe without question that it is the foreign policy of our nation, the preserving of our economic Empire that has plunged us into the

23

worldwide conflagration that we're now suffering. To be sure, we're the rich kid on the block, our system the most successful and beneficial ever devised by man. We'll naturally be envied, hated (and ironically copied longingly) for our resounding material ingenuity and triumphs.

But that, to me, is only the tip of the iceberg. Below is the rumbling and the angry payback for the violence our policies have wreaked on humanity for a half century. Policies that have been faithfully buried by the media and our government. Unless you read the small "alternative" press, our aggressive, self-serving policies are obscured. You just never hear about them. You're not supposed to hear.

Only by an entirely new policy, and by changing our approach to the world, will we ever "win" the war we're in now.

What is such a policy? Eminent political scientist Samuel P. Huntington writes: "Civilizations will have to learn to live side by side in peaceful interchange, learning from each other...mutually enriching each others' lives. The alternative is misunderstanding, tension, clash and catastrophe. In the coming era, the avoidance of major intercivilizational wars requires core states to refrain from intervening in conflicts in other civilizations."

A humanitarian approach that goes beyond the war solution. Yet where are we now? Intervening still, regardless of consequences to civilization.

Our present foreign policy identifies Iraq and Saddam Hussein as the next demon we must exorcise. Though the first President Bush once gave him a medal as our loyal ally, bought and paid for by us, ever since the Gulf War, millions of sound bytes from the government and in the media have blasted against him. We built him up as a demon in order to get massive support for the Gulf War. What do we do with our left-over anger? How do we vent it? Obviously, finish the job. This time take him down. Off him for good. Protect Israel from his missiles and dreadful weapons of mass destruction. It goes without notice that this objective is fueled by the immense money-power of the Israeli lobby over our political system.

But Israel and Saudi Arabia have those same weapons of mass destruction. So do twenty nations in the world. Get them all now? And what if they strike back? Is that really the foreign policy you and I want?

I live much of the year in the desert. We have rattlesnakes—diamondbacks, sidewinders, lethal Mohaves. But we don't have a snakebite kit. A funny thing about rattlers. The people they mainly bite are youngsters who tease them as pets, attracted to their dangerous beauty in a strange sort of way.

For the rest of us, when we see such snakes lazing on a rock or under a mesquite, we might get a shock at how truly powerful and frightening they are. I once rode my horse by accident over a diamondback as thick as my arm. He was lying stretched out in the sun, not even coiled. In a split second he had leaped six feet in the air and snapped at my boot heel.

See it from the snake's point of view. The shadow of that enormous thing above him not only ended his nap but threatened to trample him into the rocks. So instead...sure, we don't reach under rocks or into woodpiles—but always watching the desert for what might be lying on it, we simply give the snake a wide berth and leave him as he was. Unthreatened.

Isn't it possible that constant threats from something much bigger could make a Saddam Hussein snake strike out of vengeance as well as aggression?

Does our foreign policy address such eventualities? Or should we get one that does? Shouldn't we demand it?

Isn't it possible that we've risen enough in our consciousness now, and integrated ourselves enough into the broader, interconnected world to begin to realize finally that vengeance, violence, retaliatory war has never brought permanent peace?

Indeed, American military power and committed courage defeated Germany and Japan, the first axis. It finally outlasted the prior evil of communism, in forty six years of the Cold War that killed more human beings than all those who died in World War I and II combined.

What have we gained?

What is left in its wake is a new world that seems to have lost its way.

Think of that world as two massive tectonic plates. These are the systems, the cultures, the mindsets that have governed humanity for past centuries. The systems functioned, if not perfectly, still sufficiently enough to lie side by side and remain reasonably motionless.

But then in the 20th century, change trembled the world. As before, it was another of the great shifts that have wrenched human existence. Dark Ages replaced by Middle Ages. Agricultural Age replaced by Industrial Age, and before humanity could even process such a paradigm, the Information Age swept away all prior concepts. Old institutions like church and state began to become unworkable, often corrupt. They no longer were serving mankind as they once had. Decay, disintegration and raging anger began to appear worldwide. Fissures broke apart in the plates, then ominous rumbles from deep down in a yearning earth.

Some kind of an earthquake was about to happen. All the roaring and fighting between the plates was going to one day explode in catastrophe. No one knew how to head it off.

Isn't that where we are now? In the dying of the old, failed way, could it be that the violence in the earth is forming a new way, perhaps the Consciousness Age? If so, then our rising in consciousness to new mindsets is already creating the systems that will better serve the needs of all humanity.

And the final peace, the stilling of the plates in a new equilibrium, will come from our realizing at last the obvious. The human family is all one. Despite our wondrous, vital diversity, we are still a living, breathing single unit, a common and positive energy spreading out across the cosmos, and with it the possibility of a peace all mankind longs for.

Isn't that the patriot's most important mission now? To try, just once, you and I and as many Americans as possible—try taking action for peace. There are ways. There are plans. There are committed citizens already taking action. But in the roar for still more war, their voices are barely heard.

To love my country, to me, means to care enough to do my bit to try to protect it from self-inflicted harm. To shield it from arrogant passion, from "step across this line" war mentality. Instead, to edge it gently toward patient justice and mostly, compassion. From such humility and gratitude for our blessings, love can begin to lead us to the realization that we, wherever we may live, in whatever place or race, are truly all one. One bleed, all mourn. One die, all die. One hope, all hope.

This is the plea, then. Each of us, to love our country back to its original ideal: that as patriotic Americans, we shall lead mankind into the new. If we have the courage and commitment, we shall be, all of us again, what Lincoln saw in our nobility and spiritual longing, the "last best hope on earth."

Can do, we used to say in World War II.

We still can, and God willing, will.

GETTING REAL IS SHARING YOUR AWARENESS

After 9/11, the vast majority of us want to DO SOMETHING ABOUT IT.

Take action, some kind, any kind. But what? How?

Some people write letters to the kids in Afghanistan, Palestine or Iraq. Others volunteer for community service. More, perhaps, donate money to the victims of the tragedy. All great and selfless love, these expressions of sorrow and compassion.

But underpinning them all, there's a personal response anyone can make that could well be even more effective. You don't have to join anything, don't have to give money or go someplace and march with placards.

No. All you have to do is sit still, listen to the silence between your thoughts, and when you open your eyes again, look around at your world.

<u>Become aware.</u>

<u>Become aware of what's going on out there.</u> Let your heart tell you whether it's true or false.

And once you have, share your awareness with as many people as you can.

That's how change happens, and change is needed to happen, right now.

There's a good chance that women will lead the awareness crusade. They're better at it than men. As the bearers of life, they have more reverence for life. Because of their different wiring, their intuitions are more finely attuned to the human spirit and its cries of suffering.

They just don't have the male ego driving them on to perform, bring home the bacon, **DO, GET, WIN!**

This is not to say that women can't be fiendishly cruel. Cavalry troopers in the Indian wars dreaded being handed over to hostile squaws. They were the most excruciating torturers of all.

Perhaps the difference is, women rarely start wars. That's the male prerogative. To prove his true macho, doesn't he have to go conquer something?

Racetrack people have learned this. On the vast majority of horse farms, priceless colts are given to a young woman to break. Or to a gallop girl for their workouts. The reason: the usual male horse breaker is too harsh, hasty and lacking in patience. He has to <u>win</u> over the colt, show the dangerous little bastard what life is all about. The female breaker already knows and lets the colt know she knows. The young stud or filly feels this gentleness and understanding and tries to please her.

Watch bird dogs in the field. Too often, a powerful male pointer will run bolder, cover more ground, even have a superb nose. And too often, a thick head. Whistle him in? No way. His male way, his ego drives him on until he busts a covey and nobody gets a shot. He looks at you with sorry eyes and then runs on to do it again. Progress.

But the female pointer doesn't go very far away from you. There may be better birds far off someplace, but she's content to find what are here close. She walks on little cat feet, careful, smarter, finer tuned nose. And when she stops on a point, it's almost never false. She's found something there. Got 'em.

That's my little dog-girl, Lily. And maybe out of mutual admiration I've anthropomorphized her into my wife-girl, Teddy. Because they both have the same precious quality. They listen to the silence between thoughts. They are aware.

Several months after 9/11, Teddy had heard enough to want to share what she felt. She began writing how she felt about the U.S. response and sending it to family and friends:

"Our passion against the relentless war policy of our government has shifted to a sad resignation. After watching retired generals, grinning like school boys playing with potato bazookas, while discussing the fantastic devastation of daisy cutters, I wanted to stand in the living room and wail like an ancient crone and rend my garments. When I'd be gathering eggs or riding across the ranch after cows, the old sixties song, *Where Have All the Flowers Gone,* would be playing at the back of my brain. The mixture of grief and disbelief were edged with anxiety as the flags waved and the ancient war rhetoric began to roll the drums.

"There's so much in our country about which to be proud. Every American child should study the Federalist papers and understand the great leap in human consciousness the Declaration of Independence was in the 18th century, but the old patriotic reflex has always signaled slaughter. In fact, bonding together against the enemy is the very source of civilization; it is the glue that made nations and keeps them together. The scapegoat is a coalescing force, intrinsic to human behavior, not only recorded by Moses but it is the same symbol used by Buddhist monks who kicked a mahogany replica of a goat before entering the temple.

"But now we are beginning a new chapter in human history. Perhaps for the first time, everyone is un-protectable—rich and poor alike. Our enormous military might will not prevent another September 11. Glass shards cemented into the tops of walls and guards with M16s are no longer enough to shield the powerful. We are all vulnerable.

"With no political expertise, I dare not hazard a suggestion, but I think that one made in the direction of a World Tribunal with the backing of all the major nations is far preferable to Bush's fifty year war. It is evident we will eventually need an international police force to pursue and prosecute the worldwide threat of terrorists. Of course, it will mean that the US must cease scuttling and dis-empowering the UN, that we will have to give up some of our sovereignty and take a different road in our foreign policies which have alienated a multitude of people. Of course, we will have to rebuild the now bureaucratic and often inept agencies, the CIA and FBI.

"Peter Jennings of ABC has been a correspondent in many nations. 'What Americans don't understand,' he said, 'is that we are hated all over the world.' What he didn't point out is that Americans as a people, as individuals, are loved all over the world. Our generosity is unmatched, just as the freedom and opportunity we offer are unmatched anywhere. And how easy it is to lay most of the blame on envy. But when and where have people been inspired to sacrifice their lives out of envy? It is our aggressive policies that are hated. We have a long list of interference and alignment with dictators and oligarchies in order to protect our corporate interests. Why are the polices that have brought about this hatred not been examined and aired one by one in the mainstream media?

"Will we remember that hatred begets hatred, that violence begets violence, that compassion begets compassion? Perhaps we will be cornered into this realization in the ensuing decades of conflict when our economy, our blood and our psyche are drenched in frustration, failure and fear. I had hoped it would come after September 11. I pray for the transformation of enough Americans that will bring forth peace from this 'land of the free and home of the brave.'

"I pray for Bush to end a speech with, "God Bless the Human Family.""

She's still waiting for that to happen. Who isn't? But the comforting thing is, she's received many letters, calls, and e-mails, all agreeing.

As one friend said, "I read the papers differently now."

When enough of us do that, change will happen by the power of awareness—and passing it on.

New York, 1981: Ronald Reagan has just been elected President. I'm at a fancy cocktail party, Park Avenue apartment. All bigshots in the room except me. One, a prominent international financier, sidles up. "I hear you've been an old friend of Reagan's. What kind of President do you think he'll make?"

"Well," I answer, "in my experience with him, he's always been likeable and articulate. Strong in his beliefs. What you see is pretty much what you get. He's a decent guy, but whether he has the ability to run the nation and the world, I just don't know."

The financier smiles. "Exactly what we want. A patriotic figurehead up there, wave the flag. We'll take care of the rest."

"We?" I thought.

Who is we?

DIGGING OUT THE TRUTH: 1

Why were we attacked September 11th?

A year ago, Chalmers Johnson, a respected Asia specialist and author of a dozen books on foreign policy, wrote <u>Blowback: The Costs and Consequences of American Empire.</u> When asked if September 11th was an example of blowback, he replied, "Of course it is. That's exactly what my book was written for. It was a warning to my fellow Americans that our foreign policy was going to produce something like this. It's important to stress, contrary to what people in Washington and the media are saying, that this was not an attack on the United States. This was an attack on American foreign policy. It was an example of the strategies of the weak against the overwhelmingly powerful.

"Our Department of Defense invented the phrase 'collateral damage' to deal with the dead Iraqis and dead Serbs as a result of our bombings of their countries...I know it sounds cruel to say, but the people of New York were collateral damage of American foreign policy. It was inevitable that something like this would come back.

"What happened on September 11^{th,} was an almost catastrophic failure of intelligence by extremely expensive agencies that do not do anything. And so far, the American reaction seems to be to target the Bill of Rights more than anything else. Retaliation is not the answer. It hasn't worked for Israel, it has only exacerbated the situation. It won't work for us. The greatest danger we have now is militarism in America...The military will have ever greater authority in our society. We know how that will end. We're talking here about imperial overstretch, and the weakness of the imperial structure that will ultimately lead to a collapse.

"I believe," he concludes, "that there will be a public demand to make changes now in our foreign policy. If we persist in bombing innocent people in Afghanistan, then you must say we deserve what we're going to get."

But of course we don't think we deserve it. Why should we have such a tragedy brought down upon us?

When he announced the air strikes, President George W. Bush said, "We're a peaceful nation. The most free nation in the world. A nation built on fundamental values that rejects hate, rejects violence, rejects murderers and rejects evil."

The record clearly shows that we Americans are friendly, easy going, we do our best to be fair and just. We're the most churched nation in the world, God fearing, generous, the biggest donors to charities. We've put our money where our mouth is. Whether hurricane, earthquake or flood, our aid rushes in first to ease the suffering. The world knows that. No people on earth have done so much for the benefit of humanity as we have.

It's more than our technology, our ingenuity, our courage. It's the openness of our American heart, our willingness to share with all peoples the freedoms we've won the hard way and rightly hold sacred. In God we Trust. We have so much to thank God for, and we do.

Just in being the remarkable people we are, we have found our peace. We want to live at peace, but we haven't had much of it.

"In the United States' 200 plus year history," writes John Stockwell, "we have fought 15 wars." A former station chief in Angola, the Congo and up-country

Vietnam, Stockwell holds the CIA's second most coveted decoration—which he handed back when he became the highest CIA officer to resign in protest.

"We have put our military into other countries to force them to bend to our will about 200 times, or about once a year. As justification, the U.S. leaders have always cited national interests or the protection of U.S. lives or property (at the expense of the local people's lives and property.)" Invariably, we called it 'national defense.'

"Was it in our defense," asks Colman McCarthy, former Washington Post columnist and now director of the Center for Teaching Peace, "that in the last ten years Washington has sent troops to kill people or threaten to kill people in Lebanon, Grenada, Libya, Panama, the Persian Gulf, Somalia, Haiti, Sudan, Yugoslavia and Afghanistan twice? A familiar pattern has been followed, glamorize (our wars), demonize, victimize, rationalize."

Arundhati Roy, a Booker Prize-winning author from New Delhi: "Since World War II, overtly and covertly, America has been at war with: China, Korea, Guatemala, Indonesia, Cuba, the Belgian Congo, Peru, Laos, Vietnam, Cambodia, Grenada, Libya, El Salvador,

Nicaragua, Panama, Iraq, Sudan, Yugoslavia and Afghanistan."

Now, why has this happened?

Could it be what the financier told me in discussing Reagan? "Leave the rest to us." The "us," unfortunately, is not ordinary citizens like you and me. Rather, it's a skein of elite combines in politics, media, corporations and defense industries who need these wars to further or protect their own special interests.

It is a foreign policy of the few, with the many having to do the paying and dying for it.

But lately, particularly after 9/11, more and more Americans are not only waking up to the injustice of it and the enormous cost, but in a broader world view are demanding obvious changes. As political scientist Samuel P. Huntington has said, we have to learn to live side by side in peaceful interchange, "mutually enriching each others' lives."

This means detaching ourselves from the military/solution/reflex. Why should we support oligarchic, undemocratic regimes worldwide? Isn't it that we invariably back a "strong man,"—"our SOB," as

Roosevelt said about Somoza in Nicaragua—because such hard-handed rulers create a safe, stable market in which our corporations can sell their goods?

Noreiga, Saddam, binLaden were all "national security assets," financed by us to fight the threat of communism. Seen in retrospect, the Cold War, for all its ideological differences, was at its root economic. Who was going to get the vast markets of Eastern Europe, Latin America, Africa and Asia? The Soviets, or the business interests of ourselves and the West?

Now let's be clear about one thing. Despite corporate influence on our foreign and domestic politics, business itself is not a demon nor are the men and women who carry it out. They're providing an essential service not only for themselves but for the benefit of mankind.

Any responsible activist working for political change should try earnestly not to inflame by criticism, but rather to inspire. Lead toward the truth. It's the getting to "yes," the patient humility of seeing the opponent's point of view that is the most effective road to constructive solution.

In an age that demands a conspiracy behind every great action, the corporate state is no such animal. It's not a John Birch Society goblin of greedy CEO's meeting at the Yale Club and plotting how to take over America and the world. Corporate executives are some of the brightest, most creative people in the nation. They're tough and smart or they wouldn't have gotten where they are. They know what they're doing and it's to serve their bottom line. That's what they were hired for. Many of them have reached far beyond their corporate realms to establish foundations and visionary programs that benefit all Americans. They love the nation that had given them so much, and they mean to give back, in gratitude. In the composite of these executives, there is a *zeitgeist* of progress and a mind-set that is common to most of them. They've learned the hard way what works and what doesn't work. Thus, when they're confronted with some national or international problem, they often react the same way. They're not out to steal the country, only to better it. Then they go back to fighting each others' fiefdoms for market share. They're in the political battleground to—crudely—cover their ass. That's their only conspiracy—and in the amalgam of their balance sheets, they have immense power. They don't intend to give it up.

Also, the majority of politicians I've known are dedicated people. To serve the country, they've given up precious time with their families. They lose out on job opportunities at home. They work very hard, and it's not just for the ego-stroking, the influence or the power in it. These men and women honestly want to make a better country, but they're trapped in a brutal money-system. Some representatives actually call their big donors "clients." Mondays and Fridays in Congress are often devoted to fund-raising for re-election. If the peoples' representatives don't go along with the owners wishes, they go home.

In addition to checking the corporate money/power influence on our foreign policy, our support of oligarchs or our meddling in the governments of other nations must also be ended. Much of it has been implemented by the CIA. Therefore, detachment to "peaceful interchange" must also begin with a re-structuring and re-direction of the CIA, which one agent has called "capitalism's invisible army."

As agent John Stockwell testified to Congress: "The Church Committee in 1975 revealed that (up to then) CIA had run 3000 major covert operations and over 10,000 minor operations—all illegal, and all designed to disrupt, destabilize or modify the activities of other countries.

"Coming to grips with these US/CIA activities is very difficult, but adding them up as best we can, we come up with a figure of six million people killed—and this is a minimum figure. (Civilian 'collateral damage') Included are one million killed in the Korean War, two million killed in the Vietnam War, 800,000 killed in Indonesia, one million killed in Cambodia, twenty thousand killed in Angola—the operation I was part of—and twenty-two thousand killed in Nicaragua. These people would not have died if U.S. tax dollars had not been spent by the CIA to inflame tensions, finance covert political and military activity, and destabilize societies."

The way many of them were killed, Stockwell continues, was gruesome beyond belief. Latin American death squads, trained by us at our School of the Americas at Ft. Benning, Georgia, have repeatedly performed unspeakable atrocities, wiping out whole villages of Indians down even to the last child.

Today, Thanksgiving 2001, I have just seen my 7ᵗʰ grandchild, two days old. She's tiny, 5 lbs., she's beautiful, her face a work of art, her eyes opening to innocence, wonder, trust. A child like that on a bayonet, with U.S. stamped on it?

The School of the Americas provided military manuals for the Latin American trainees, teaching them torture and assassination techniques. Against documented evidence, Congress voted down a bill to terminate the School.

Again, our corporate economy wants stable markets. Goon squads provide it. A new world view will end such barbarity and make illegal our support of it.

How, for example, can we justify what the *contras* did in Nicaragua? Also trained and armed by the U.S., they made a practice of coming into small towns and selecting a family for punishment. The children were dragged outside to watch as *contras* castrated their father, raped their mother and cut off her breasts. At one point in the "war," Ronald Reagan said proudly, "I am a *contra*."

Under Somoza, whom the U.S. supported for years, Nicaragua was a miserable, brutal dictatorship. When the Sandinistas took over and were democratically elected, Washington reacted in horror. The beards, the wild propaganda, the combat dungarees—it was Castro all over again, a possible Soviet base within hours from our border. Ignored in the hysteria was the fact that in the 20th century, the U.S. had been to war three times in Nicaragua, fighting to protect what we regarded as our economic turf, which now a revolutionary rabble was threatening to take away. However erratically, the Sandinistas were giving land back to the people, giving them medical care, dramatically raising their literacy levels and providing amnesty to Somoza's goon squads.

It wasn't enough. The threat was perceived as being too great. The U.S. spent $1 billion dollars to transform

Nicaragua from a struggling but then hopeful nation into the most ravaged, poorest country in our hemisphere.

"CIA destabilizations," Stockwell writes, "kill people who never were our enemies—that's not the problem—but to leave behind for each one of the dead perhaps five loved ones who are now traumatically conditioned to violence and hostility against the United States. This ensures that the world will continue to be a violent place, justifying our endless production of arms to 'defend' ourselves in a violent world."

Isn't it time to expose the real reasons for our war-making, and take action to end domination of our foreign policy by special interests?

When a crusty old ranch gal in Wyoming read my article, she shot back: "I'll give you the reason why we do it, mister. One word. Spell it out: M-O-N-E-Y."

Bonita, AZ, 1990: two young men come out to the ranch to hunt. They're U.S. captains, West Pointers, combat veterans, one in the Air Force, another in Army infantry. These seasoned junior officers are the vital future of our military. But both have just resigned their commissions. When I ask why, they say, "We chose the military as a career. Our understanding was that our mission was to defend the United States. But that's not true anymore. We're being used to defend the American economic empire overseas. That's not what we signed on for. We gave them back our bars and opted out."

Guadalcanal, 1944: I'm flying as a co-pilot and navigator on the personal aircraft of Major General Roy S. Geiger, USMC. He commands half the Marines in the Pacific. Sometimes on our flights with him or in a soggy tent waiting for the rain to stop, the Old Man lights up a cigar and reminisces gruffly about his pre-war service in the China Horse Marines and in the Banana Wars of Central America. Here, he and other Marines pioneered not only jungle fighting techniques but primitive dive bombing. Once and a while, he'll tell some story about the banty, feisty commander he'd had in those days, "old Smedley."

This legendary hero of the Marine Corps, General Smedley D. Butler was a two-time Medal of Honor winner. From the Boxer Rebellion of 1900 on up, he'd fought in much of the world. In the 1930's, he said in a speech:

"I spent most of my career being a high-class muscleman for Big Business, for Wall Street and the bankers...in short, I was a racketeer, a gangster for capitalism. I helped make Mexico safe for American oil interests in 1914...made Haiti and Cuba a decent place for the National City Bank boys to collect revenues in. The best Al Capone had was three districts. I operated on three continents."

For telling the truth, General Butler was placed under house arrest and virtually drummed out of the Marine Corps.

In evaluating how to reach peaceful interchange with other nations and enriching each others' lives, one has to go back to the evolution of our Republic into an Empire. Now, of course, it's obvious that the world is totally intertwined. This is why we have slogans like "New

World Order." It *is* new, and we have joined it. We must. The reasons are valid and also historical. Our products and ingenuity are demanded all over the world. We have enriched the lives of millions and have profited from it, too, as well we should. We've enhanced our corporations and our lifestyles at home. That all makes sense. The question is: do we have to keep doing it ruthlessly, or will a new world view put the human equation back into our actions? That means a change in economic and foreign policy, and an understanding of how ours were formed and led us to where we are today.

Our American thrust toward Empire actually began in 1845. We went in, defeated Mexico and snatched what's now California and the Southwest. The Mexicans were a brave but comic opera army—imperialism always works better when you've got a weaker opponent. Henry David Thoreau, the lanky idealist of Walden Pond was so shocked that he wrote an essay about it, "On Civil Disobedience." He was the first conscientious objector to war, and for his trouble was slammed into jail by the government. Thoreau was echoing George Washington who warned our weak and tottering nation to "avoid foreign entanglements." After all, most Americans had fled the royal wars of imperial Europe, the endless intrigues. We had no stomach ever again to hurl ourselves into bloodbaths beyond our blessed shores.

So we founded a Republic whose ideal was to defend us at home and prosper us. From the Civil War's end and onward, we flowered in invention, growth, culture and amazing accomplishments. But by the 1890's, not only had we conquered our last frontier but our country had succeeded so well that Teddy Roosevelt was inspired to say: "America's ability to produce manufactured goods will soon outstrip her capacity to consume them. The only thing we can depend on is sea power. If we have it, we have the world."

In short, we'd outgrown ourselves. Control the seas and we could go anywhere. The world needed us and our products. Give the lady what she wants.

Henry James called T.R. "the very embodiment of noise." And the British Ambassador, reporting to Whitehall: "We must never forget that the President is seven years old." But when the battleship Maine blew up in Havana under suspicious circumstances, Teddy and

William Randolph Hearst got their "splendid little war." Lost in the flag-waving of the moment was the bottom line, the reason why, as thundered out on the Senate floor by Albert Beveridge of Indiana. "God has made us the master organizers of the world. We are the adepts who must administer government to savage and senile peoples. God has marked the American people his chosen nation to finally lead in the regeneration of the world."

Three years ago, defending our use of cruise missiles against Iraq, Secretary of State Madeline Albright said: "If we have to use force, it is because we are America. We are the indispensable nation. We stand tall. We see further into the future."

As novelist-historian Gore Vidal reports, "President McKinley decided we ought to keep the Philippines in order to Christianize the natives. When reminded that Filipinos were already Roman Catholic, the President responded: 'Exactly.' So we betrayed the Filipino nationalists and began our own conquest.

"Unsurprisingly, reenactment films from the time chose not to dwell on the slaughter of some 200,000

Filipino men, women and children. But Mark Twain did salute our act of genocide by suggesting that "we replace the stars and stripes in our flag with the skull and crossbones."

Years later, when we hurled ourselves into the Banana Wars of Central America, we used the excuse that we were trying to bring those poor people freedom, democracy and good government. "But stripped of all the Presidential rhetoric," Vidal adds, "the flag followed the banks. The President was simply chief enforcer for the great financial interests."

New York, 1976: I'm having a drink with a former Secretary of State and a high-profile banker. There's been a new incident of violence in the Middle East. Arab versus Jew. Saudi Arabia may be threatened. I ask: "If this leads to a war, what are we going to do?"

"Do?" thunders the ex-Secretary. "Why, we go in with troops. We take all those countries out."

"It's our oil," says the banker.

No secret in that, claims our present foreign policy. If everything is "ours," regardless of where it exists on earth, then aren't we justified to follow the bidding of U.S. and transnational corporations to protect and deliver them their goods, by force if necessary? How did it happen that corporations have been allowed to exert such power over our political system? Isn't this something that a new world view must change?

Writes editor Michael Lind in <u>Harpers</u>: "It's against the rules to talk about a rapacious American oligarchy, and the suggestion that a small group of people with the most money and power just *might* be responsible to some degree for what has been happening to the country over the past 20 years."

Why the secret of the controlling elite doesn't get out, Lind claims, is that every time a politician from the left or the right proposes to "speak for the many," the nation's "better newspapers (<u>Washington Post, New York Times, Wall Street Journal</u>) react in "wrath and denial, claiming demagoguery." Yes, the pundits admit, economic and social inequality have been growing in the United States with alarming results, but the ruling and possessing class cannot be blamed because, well, there is no ruling possessing class.

"The American oligarchy," he concludes, "spares no pains in promoting the belief that it does not exist, but the success of its disappearing act depends on equally strenuous efforts on the part of an American public anxious to believe in egalitarian fictions and unwilling to see what is hidden in plain sight."

In 1996, U.S. corporations donated $2 billion to political campaigns. The figure is probably considerably higher now.

"American corporations aren't even subtle about it," writes Ralph Nader. "Waving a flag and carrying a big shovel, corporate interests are scooping up government benefits and taxpayer money in an unprecedented fashion while the public is preoccupied with the September 11th attacks and the war in Afghanistan."

With only a few dissenting votes, the House of Representatives rushed through a bill that would make the corporations eligible for $25 billion in tax refunds. "The bill appears," writes Washington correspondent

Charles Bartlett, "as if it were written by corporate lobbyists."

The corporations are also seeking a retroactive refund for the Alternative Minimum Tax they've paid since 1986. This tax was put in by the Reagan administration, Nader continues, "to prevent profitable corporations from escaping all tax liability through various loopholes."

Who are the recipients of the giveaways? IBM $1.4 billion, General Motors $883 million, General Electric $671 million, Daimler-Chrysler $600 million, Chevron-Texaco $572 million. In addition, disgraced and disastrous Enron was slated to receive $800 million. Who knows what for, possibly executive golden parachutes when they were bailing out on their shareholders. Not only was Enron the largest corporate donor to George W. Bush's presidential campaign, but during it gave him full use of an Enron company jet.

"The 14 biggest beneficiaries of the minimum tax repeal," writes Nader, "gave $14,769,785 in 'soft money' to the national committees of the Democratic and Republican parties in recent years. Just these 14 companies would receive $6.3 billion of the tax refund."

As national commentator Bill Moyers puts is: "The corporations are counting on you to stand at attention with your hand over your heart, pledging allegiance to the flag, while they pick your pocket."

There has always been greed, and even a new worldview can't remake those subject to it. But in the mass, a rising consciousness can and will empower enough citizens to outrage. That alone will force the political change needed to legislate long-overdue restrictions so that corporate power can no longer dominate ordinary citizens lives.

Perhaps it's enough to see the macho mentality that thrives on war, and then look at what it really means to those who have to fight or die for it.

Lake Forest, Illinois, 1942: my last night before going off to war. A man I greatly admire, World War I hero and the esteemed chairman of a transnational corporation, hugs me in a boozy fog and gives me a wincing punch on my arm: "Get one for me, boy!"

One what? The head of a "Jap" to hang on the wall?
A good job in the corporation after the war? A couple of
years later, I see some "ones." We've landed our plane on
Guam hours after crazed, drunken Japanese troops have
launched a thousand man banzai attack against Marines
dug in on Orote Point. The Marines called in every gun
on shore and in the fleet. Orote Point exploded in flame.
Vegetation torched, gone, humans gone. There they lay in
the mud and blood, an arm here, lumps of torsos and
puddles of brains there, a severed head with coconut flies
eating the death-opened eyes. Maggots feasting on dead
flesh. "Ones."

In 1973 I go back to Guam. Had to see it again. On
Orote Point, where I had stepped over hunks of Japanese
bodies, now a garrison U.S. Navy had built a
supermarket and paved the slaughter site with ball
diamonds, tennis courts and tract houses. As for the
bomb-pocked airstrip where we'd lived for uncounted
days in our plane, beside a concrete bunker reeking with
incinerated Japanese bodies—only a grassy knoll remains.

The Orote I knew, gone. Beyond in the harbor, skeletons claw at the sky: groaning cranes and drydocks that are readying our fleet to attack our latest enemies in Vietnam. On the horizon, overlooking the bloody invasion beaches rise clusters of gleaming white hotels. "American?" I ask my cab driver. He shakes his head. "They're all either owned or operated by Japs. It's their favorite honeymoon resort. They come here by the thousands."

So what had we won in our suffering and sacrifice? Instead of ridding ourselves of the Japanese "demons," we'd married them.

As I wrote in my article, back in 1945, we Americans were the envy of the world, strong in our hearts, afraid of nothing, proud of ourselves and our nation.

A short five years later, in 1950, when novelist William Faulkner received the Nobel Prize, he asked plaintively: "What has happened to the American Dream? We dozed and it abandoned us, and in the vacuum no longer sound the strong loud voices, unafraid."

After the September 11th attack, <u>Time</u> magazine ran an essay titled: "The case for rage and retaliation."

Bougainville, Guam, Pelelieu, Okinawa, 1943-1945. The only rage I remember is: how long they gotta keep us out on this stinkin' rock? The only retaliation: pity the poor bastards we had to slaughter, them and us. Please God, quit this obscenity, lift us out of the mud and blood and get us the hell home!

Flying around the Solomon Islands in 1943, we rarely see a single old beat-up U.S. destroyer. The rest are sunk. But flying home in 1945, in the thousands of miles between Okinawa and Pearl Harbor, we're never out of sight of an American ship. God, the pride brings tears to our eyes. Look what our magnificent country has done for us! We'd won the world. Peace now, forever.

We were still under the delusion, I think—at least I was—that our Republic was a true democracy where each one of us had an equal voice in deciding our policies. Only in the gradual shift from Republic to Empire did we learn that it was no longer true.

Noam Chomsky, the MIT professor whom the New York Times once called "the most important intellectual alive," writes: "The decisions that guide the destiny of the United States are primarily made by the business community and other allied elites." Gore Vidal calls them "our managers." This political or ruling class, Chomsky estimates, is probably 20% of our population. The other 80%, journalist Walter Lippman called "spectators of the action. The bewildered herd."

"The doctrinal system," Chomsky writes, "serves to divert the masses and reinforce the basic social values: passivity, submissiveness to authority, the overriding virtue of greed and personal gain, lack of concern for others, fear of real or imagined enemies, etc. The goal is to keep the bewildered herd bewildered. It's unnecessary for them to trouble themselves with what's happening in the world. In fact, it's undesirable—if they see too much reality, they may set themselves to change it."

John Jay, a signer of the Constitution, said, "The people who own the country ought to run it."

This was logical at the time. The Founding Fathers were all landowners, men of property. White men. Women and people of color were considered ineligible to make decisions. Virtually non-persons. The new nation was shaky enough that the founders didn't dare let it get out of their control and into the hands of a mostly illiterate rude, brutish rabble. So, basically, that original mindset of who should have power has continued throughout our history.

Our archaic congressional districts were laid out in geographic miles: how far a representative could ride a horse in one day. They haven't changed much to the present day. What is different now is the magnitude of the controlling information. Instead of communicating with the populace by word of mouth or by the penny newspapers the few literates could read, today's massively powerful communication system can sell national policies so totally that the "bewildered herd" not only doesn't question them, but eventually convinces itself that everybody's endorsing those policies.

U.S. media prides itself on "balance." Democratic free speech, every citizen with the right to his or her own voice. A survey taken after the Gulf War showed that the major TV networks ran 738 interviews with experts discussing the war. Against their combined opinion, the networks ran 1 interview with a representative of a major peace group. The "balance": 737-1.

Once, The <u>New York Times</u> revered Noam Chomsky as our leading intellectual. When, as a veteran political analyst he began questioning the loss of our democracy, the <u>Times</u> would not review his many works or permit his name to be mentioned.

The French have an expression: "If you don't do politics, politics will do you."

Less than half of Americans vote.

A California grocery chain printed on its shopping bags: "Don't vote. It only encourages *them*."

Since the beginnings of community life anywhere, most of humanity has always been too occupied in earning their daily bread or simply staying alive to have the time or interest to pay attention to how they're being governed. To become an active, committed citizen, one has to know what our country means, do the fascinating exploration through the grandeur of American history.

How do we know what we are now if we don't know what brought us here?.

Jackson, Wyoming, 2001: I'm interested in one of my granddaughter's education. She's gone to an excellent prep school and is now finishing up at Wellesley, an outstanding women's college. How much U.S. history, I ask? "One brief and fuzzy course years ago." Nothing more? "That was it."

But it wasn't like that always. A century ago, the U.S. had all kinds of strong, populist opposition. Some were self-educated, others highly intellectual. They *knew* their American history. All were dedicated to democracy, fiery men and women who bucked the system, whether for women's voting rights, child labor laws, fair wages in worker-protective unions. There were many bloody, noble fights in our history to win such advances for the ordinary citizen. But as the media coalesced into the single party line of corporate America, America, Inc., the voices of protest grew weaker and weaker. They had no way to get an alternative message out to the people.

Yesterday has become a void for most of our young. When someone asked me to write an update for TV on John F. Kennedy's <u>Profiles in Courage</u>, I was warned that I couldn't use any of the courageous individuals he'd profiled from out of our history. They were either all dead or forgotten in the 30-something audience's blank stare: "Who he?" No, I'd better stick to NOW people or at most someone on <u>The Lives of the Rich and Famous</u> yesterday, which was about as far back as an audience was able to remember.

Into this muddy soup of not knowing what we used to be or what we are now, the tectonic plates of our rumbling, changing world flood us with the signs and symbols of globalization. Yes, it's happening. We like their Hondas and they like our Fords. My jeans were made in Malaysia, this computer in Mexico. So indeed, we're all coming together beneficially. But if that's true, why do we have these incessant wars? Does globalization actually require that we have to rush off to some far away land to fight others just so that the New World Order gets one more orderly market for our corporations?

As somebody said, "Do we have to be the world's cop?"

Well, think about it. England, Germany, Italy, France and Japan all have powerful name-brand transnational corporations operating world-wide. The difference is, they do not have 250 military bases spanning all the continents, or a Department of Defense owning more foreign real estate than the land area of Kentucky. They do not have fleets in every ocean, a meddlesome CIA or a foreign policy staffing our alliances with some of the most murderous thugs on earth.

How come we get that job? Again, corporate influence. If civilians, as they did in Okinawa, launch bloody riots against our military occupation since 1945, our foreign policy *meisters* really don't care that a few of the natives are restless. Because, after all, others of those natives are getting a real and much appreciated handout from Uncle Sam.

Employment in our military bases. Nine hundred locals work for a single U.S. airbase in Germany, and this is one of the smallest. Naturally, U.S. servicemen are their best buddies. Yankee, please don't go home. Because why? If we did, at that point our military alliance allies would have to pick up the tab themselves for their own defense.

In the now 400 billion yearly defense budget, does the citizen taxpayer realize he's paying for this kind of foreign aid? Does he want to? If not, he better change it by closing up unneeded military shops worldwide and bringing our soldiers home, to defend us where we live.

There's a quirky corollary in our "drug problem." By going to "war" against drugs, making them fiercely illegal and out of sight expensive, what we've really done is not to win, never to win, but rather to enrich Latin drug lords on the astronomic profits they're making. What do they do with their billions? Well, some of it, for example in Mexico, goes into building beach resorts, condos and massive developments. These are a great thing for the poverty-stricken locals. They employ thousands of people.

But what about the American people who pay for it in our 21 billion a year failed drug war? Do you and I loyal citizens really want our tax dollars used in this kind of reverse-English foreign aid? Doubtful. Why not declare victory and go home? Legalize. Make drugs cheap and paying U.S. taxes, so we get paid, not the gunsels with their haciendas, fancy ladies and private armies.

Perhaps partly out of our innate American good-heartedness, but mostly, I suspect, out of a sort of guilt complex for our worldwide ravaging in "business wars," we find it more palatable to call them "humanitarian."

On paper, U.S. policy is to spread democracy to less fortunate nations, bettering the rude, brutish and short lives of their peoples. In certain cases, this has been accomplished. Americans are natural humanitarians. Unfortunately, there are times, U.S. leaders have admitted, when "a few eggs have to be broken to make the omelet." People will have to be killed to keep them from killing other people. But the end result will be worth it—at least to the bottom line.

TV, USA, 2001: footage of burly GI's coddling native babies, tons of U.S. food parachuting down to Afghan people. Gleeful Afghan women, tearing off their Taliban veils. Liberation. That's our humanitarian role. Thank God for our brave, big-hearted kids who risk their lives to do it.

"As a gesture of humanitarian support," writes author Arundhati Roy from New Delhi, "the U.S. says it plans to drop 500,000 food packets. That will still add up to only a single meal for half a million people out of the several million in dire need of food. Aid workers have condemned it as a cynical, dangerous public relations exercise. They say that air dropping food packets is worse than futile. The food will never get to those who really need it. More dangerous, those who run out to retrieve the packets will risk being blown up by land mines. A tragic alms race.

"Nevertheless, the food packets had a photo-op all to themselves. After three years of unrelenting drought, an air-dropped airline meal in Jalalabad! The level of cultural ineptitude, the failure to understand what months of relentless hunger and grinding poverty *really* mean, the U.S. government's attempt to use even this abject misery to boost its self-image beggars description.

"Put your ear to the ground in this part of the world, and you can hear the thrumming, the deadly drumbeat of burgeoning anger. *Please, please,* stop the war now! Enough people have died. The smart missiles are just not smart enough. They're blowing up whole warehouses of suppressed fury."

Okinawa, 1945. Okinawa is General Geiger's operation. One morning, I go up with him to watch Marines storming a burial tomb. By tradition, it's shaped like female genitalia, the protective concrete roof simulating the womb, and the narrow exit door being the mouth of the vagina. Life would be born through here. Only now it won't. Death pumps in from the nozzle of a flamethrower. Can't blame these grim, war weary Marines. They think Japanese snipers have holed up in the tomb. They do it all the time.

What comes out, though, are only two uniforms in flames, 14-15 year old terrified Okinawan kids conscripted by the Japanese. Behind them come maybe 40 Okinawan civilians, old men, women, children, black pajamas hanging in burning shards. Seared flesh, crawling or hobbling hamburgers. One little kid, his chest bleeding and smoking, begins to whimper. His burned mother slaps him to make him brave and leads him past us with hatred in her eyes.

But we didn't know! How could we have known? General Geiger doesn't watch it either. The cost of war. They did it to us, collateral damage is inevitable. More to the point, how many thousands of his own boys has he lost in all his wars? The fifth Marine aviator, he's been fighting and flying all over the world since before the first World War. In charge of all aviation at Guadalcanal, he virtually saved the island. But then came his ground command in the abattoirs of Bougainville, Guam, Pelelieu and finally this biggest off all, Okinawa. In the beginning, he had two Doberman war dogs. They'd leap up against his chest and he'd play with them, robust and daring, a tough guy still in his prime. In the seventeen months I've been with him, I watch the strain of command wear him down until the dogs would leap and almost knock him down at Okinawa. Here he's already lost the most Marines of his career. He grieves each one. Tries to write their families, but lately now there are so many, he just shoves the envelope at me in his gruff way: "Answer, Carney." I do my best. He never looks at my replies, just scrawls his name.

But, that day at the tomb, as we move away, our medics are gently caring for the Okinawan civilians, sulfa packs, burn cream. A Marine or two kneel among the kids and give them K-ration packs that have candy in them, Lucky Strikes and a stick of Wrigley's Spearmint gum.

Our tender humanitarianism was touching and eloquent in the "Good War" Number II, a compassionate counterpart to its actual horror. But what of now? When corpo-power links economic and military objectives into a single strategic scramble, it's not only hard for the citizen to tell the players without a scorecard, but there is a distinct feeling that nobody is keeping score at all. As Abbott and Costello used to say, "Who's on first? No, who is on second, What is on first."

Do we really deserve a foreign policy that leaps from sound byte to sound byte with no foreseeable end in sight?

"Afghanistan has been substituted for terrorism," writes William Pfaff in the <u>International Herald Tribune</u>, "because Afghanistan is accessible to military power. The employment of high tech munitions against irrelevant targets is not only unjust but is a distraction from measures that actually deal with the terrorist threat. Washington might take the time to reflect on its responsibility, which is to deal intelligently with the terrorist threat to the United States. Washington has cast BinLaden as the personification of evil. But he and his group are merely instances of that threat. If he is killed, he will be replaced. The causes of terrorism will remain, and they are political. Afghanistan and its people are no threat to the United States, but they are the ones taking the full weight of America's indignation. The Administration's priorities are upside down."

In all the globalization since the end of World War II, the hope of many Americans, myself included, was that our foreign aid represented a truly generous contribution to world welfare and peace. Also good business. If we raised the standards of living everywhere, those people would not only be better off but would make us better off because they'd buy our goods.

Well, look at some unintended consequences. When IMF, GATT and NAFTA were fast-tracked through our Congress, so fast that few legislators and almost no citizens could even understand what they said, nobody could fast-forward to get a look at the havoc they'd wreak in the host nations.

In factories on the U.S. border, American and foreign name brand corporations pay Mexican girls $4 a day. These maquila workers live in cardboard shacks bordering rivers of raw sewage. They have been subject to rape, murder, and at least in one case, due to industrial pollution, a mother's baby was born without a brain. Another transnational paid a U.S. sports star more for one TV commercial than it pays its 75,000 Indonesian girls for working a year.

"These corporations are destroying their own resource base, their own businesses and they can't see it. There is nobody at the helm."

So says Allan Savory, a former military and political hero in Zimbabwe and the founder of Holistic Range Management. This program, now being used worldwide, is dedicated to preserving the earth's resources and helping the cultures to a new mindset so that they can survive in their natural environment.

"Corporate economic might and muscle seeking short term profits and goals is unwittingly damaging and undermining nation states, democracies and cultures worldwide. There's nothing wrong with capitalism. There is everything wrong with its ugly side because it is causing such global anger.

"There are corporations now with budgets far larger than most countries, and the market they are leading never, ever looks at anything but the dollar bottom line. It never looks at the social and environmental consequences, and there is no global electorate that can vote against it or in any way control what is happening.

"America's governments," he concludes, "have had a track record of destroying fledgling democracies and supporting dictators who would favor corporate profits and interests. American governments have stood by and watched genocide, but reacted immediately when their oil was threatened."

When religious people are raped or murdered in America's "plantation colonies," the U.S. government slaps a few wrists, but basically its military advisers look the other way. Presently, U.S. helicopters and armed forces are waging war across Latin America, intending to napalm it clean in the U.S. Drug War.

Against this background, American Foreign Aid programs are intended to be generous, idealistic compensation. But look at it more closely.

"After the U.S. attack on Noreiga in Panama," writes Noam Chomsky, "I happened to run the numbers on it. Bush gave this magnanimous aid to Panama—a billion dollars after we destroyed the economy and then wiped the place out. Then you look at what the newspapers didn't report. What is this billion dollars in aid? Four hundred million of it, forty percent, is incentives for U.S. business to export to Panama, so it's a purchase of U.S. goods. What that means is 40% of it is a gift from the American taxpayer to American business, and about another hundred million is export-import bank guarantees which are another form of subsidy to American business. Most of the rest is payoffs to banks. It's called 'stabilizing the economy,' but if you take it apart, it's paying off the bank loans taken by the Panamanian government during the period when the United States was crushing and destroying their economy."

Again, these are old wars, all but forgotten in our current rush to a new one. Not only has the Bush Administration targeted an "Axis of Evil," old favorites, North Korea, Iran and Iraq, but now a leaked Pentagon document has virtually spelled out the unthinkable. The President says himself that he wants "all options." Meaning, in the nuclear priesthood document, targeting with nuclear weapons not only the above demons, but Libya, Sudan and—in the broadest possible reach of some Pentagon Dr. Strangelove's imagination—targeting as well the Soviet Union and China.

Richard Nixon risked political suicide to bring China back into the civilized world. Ronald Reagan took a brave step to de-nuclearize our standoff with the Soviets, and to de-fang the Evil Empire into human beings just like ourselves.

And now, did that all go out the window? Is it nukes again? Is that the foreign policy American citizens want? But it's still being used, very much so, in the roaring threat-war against Saddam Hussein and Iraq.

What are the facts behind it?

According to Hans von Sponeck, former UN coordinator for Iraq, "All decent people will feel American after September 11th. But we must remind ourselves: a World Trade Center incident happens every month in Iraq when 5000 children die of malnutrition and disease. The UN estimates that more than a million Iraqis have died due, directly or indirectly, to 11 years of sanctions."

Von Sponeck acknowledged that Saddam Hussein has contributed to the suffering of his people, and that it makes sense to fear a despot with such an abusive human rights record. "But Americans," he adds, "suffer from 'political amnesia,' forgetting that the Iraqi dictator is not a 'self-made man.' The U.S. should not be so self-righteous about Saddam, after backing him for a decade in Iraq's war with Iran."

Our sanctions have so crippled Iraq that Saddam only has enough revenue now to allocate $252 per person to its 22 million citizens. Figures verified by the UN, CARE, CARITAS and the Red Cross show—

"—147 Iraqi parents lose a child to death each day

—incidents of child and adult cancers are widespread in areas close to Basra where U.S. forces used depleted uranium during the Gulf War.

—one in five children suffer from malnutrition.

—contamination of water systems and lack of repair equipment has helped to spread diarrhea, typhoid and cholera for which there are insufficient medicines to cure.

—literacy rates which were 80% in 1985 have fallen to 58% in 1995.

—37% of school buildings are too dangerous for use as a result of damage inflicted by the Gulf War.

—Iraqi medical schools which once trained many foreign doctors have not been allowed to obtain new textbooks, research articles or medical journals in 11 years.

—in a nation that once prized 'gender-balanced' education, only a trickle of girls attend schools as their parents lack the money to educate both boys and girls.

—the national unemployment rate is estimated at between 60 and 75%.

"I have never seen more people crying, sitting staring or unable to cope," von Sponeck added. "It is a scandal that the international community allowed this punitive action to happen."

What about Saddam being a demon "worse than Hitler," and possessing nuclear and biological weapons? Von Sponeck, after 17 months in the field in Iraq, rejects the nuclear and biological threat. "Where is the evidence?" he asks. When former Secretary of Defense William Cohen met with incoming President Bush on

January 10th this year, Cohen stated: "Iraq no longer poses a military threat to the United States."

But please note: every time a TV host or his interviewee mention Saddam Hussein, they always tie him to biological or nuclear weapons. Build the fear necessary to justify our attack.

"U.S. media," vonSponeck writes, "is full of disinformation, distortion and misinterpretation, much of it emanating from the State Department. It is easier," he concludes, "to demonize an enemy than to get the facts."

William Pfaff of the <u>International Herald Tribune</u> calls it "Washington's Manichaean formulation of war against evil, which by definition can never be won." BinLaden is the latest example. "The gross exaggerations of the American government," he continues, "in attributing to him global subversive powers explain in part why the attacks on the World Trade Center and the Pentagon were such traumatic events for Americans. They were taken as demonstrations that it was all true!

"Administration officials and the policy community nevertheless relentlessly went on, speculating on where Quaida would strike next, repeatedly issuing and debating warnings of unspecified new terrors. Now BinLaden, the reimagined Dr. No, the reanimated Dr. FuManchu, the new Yellow Peril is seen shaking his fists and promising the destruction of the United States itself—while fleeing for his own life."

For the citizen to dig out the truth of the Middle East mess, not only does one have to understand the lethal web of political/corporate/military and defense industry power, but also to unearth the wriggling fingers of lobbies who are pulling some very important and (threatening to us) political strings. Again, money talks.

Since its inception, the U.S. has given Israel more aid than any other nation, $3 billion this year, in a total of $80 billion thus far. But instead of buying goods from corporations to give to other countries, the U.S. pays Israel in cash. Washington insiders have long claimed that these recycled dollars are used by Israeli lobbies to influence our elections.

"If the pro-Israel bias of the American government was a factor in the September 11th attack," writes Charles Bartlett, a Pulitzer prize-winning Washington correspondent, "Bush has been cautious in moving to correct it. Secretary Powell was prepared, we understand, to propose immediate negotiations and press harder on Israel to abandon its occupation of the West Bank but he was restrained by the White House. One report in the Israeli press has it that his speech was altered 38 times. He was not, for instance, allowed to talk of a 'shared Jerusalem.' (Now, finally, the Administration has found the courage to seek, via the UN, a separate Palestinian state. ED)

"Bush," Bartlett continues, "is dealing with members of Congress, conservative and liberal, who defer in every instance to Israeli interests. This week's <u>Jerusalem Post</u> writes: 'AIPAC and other pro-Israel lobbying groups are feared, if not always loved on Capitol Hill. Any politician with national ambitions must consider the heavy concentration of Jews in states rich in electoral votes and the wildly disproportionate Jewish money contributed to campaigns.'

"These dynamics are evident," Bartlett says, "in talks by Democrats already competing for the 2002 party nomination: Joe Biden, Joe Liberman and John Kerry. They urge that Bush shift the focus of his anti-terrorist hostility to Iraq. This would serve Israel's purpose of diverting administration pressures away from the Middle East." (And, if the U.S. can be persuaded to blow away Iraq next, this would remove Israel's greatest threat at the moment. ED.)

"Similarly," Bartlett continues, "98 senators petitioned the White House to do nothing to impair Israel's position. The first Congressional delegation to warn against any shift of policy against Israel was a group of right-wingers led by Rep. Tom DeLay. They are far more interested in political money than they are in Israel."

The good news is—and it should be noted—that there are signs of unease in American Jews. Edgar Bronfman, who heads the World Jewish Congress Assembly declared in a recent speech in Jerusalem that it is time "for Israel to get back on the moral high ground," to withdraw from Gaza, to abandon indefensible settlements, and to settle its security issues by plebiscite, not by votes in the Knesset. "Although derided in the Israeli media," Bartlett adds, "as improper counsel from a Jew living abroad, it was noted that the strategic interests of American and Israeli Jews "are not now exactly the same."

The last puzzle in the Middle Eastern mess that the citizen has to try to put together is the "our oil" concept. Is the protection of our oil why we're rushing toward war in the region?

Nina Burleigh, formerly of <u>Time</u>, was one of the first American journalists to enter Iraq after the Gulf War. "Afghanistan, she says, "happens to be situated in the middle of that perennial vital interest—abundant oil. By 2050, Central Asia will account for more than 80% of our oil. On September 10th, the <u>Oil and Gas Journal </u>reported that Central Asia represents one of the last great frontiers, offering opportunities for investment in the discovery, production, transportation and refining of enormous quantities of oil and gas reserves.

"It's assumed that we need unimpeded access to 'The Stans' for our geologists, construction workers and pipelines if we are going to realize the fossil-free future outlined by Vice-President Cheney. A number of pipeline projects have been proposed—all within reach of the Taliban thugs, and could be much safer by American vanquishment of Muslim terrorism.

"It doesn't add up to a conspiracy theory. But it does mean there is a significant MONEY subtext that the American public ought to know about as 'Operation Enduring Freedom' blasts new holes where pipelines might someday be buried."

Vice-President Cheney, long an oil company lawyer, was before his election chairman of Halliburton, one of the world's largest oil field service companies. President George Bush and President George W. Bush were both in the oil business. Interestingly, Halliburton and Enron were the largest recipients of contracts to rebuild our ally Kuwait because of its destruction in the Gulf War.

"Father Bush," continues Nina Burleigh, "the former President and CIA Director specializes in Asia, and has been in and out of Saudi Arabia and Kuwait (countries that revere him thanks to the Gulf War) often since his presidency."

"Few of us doubt," writes Indian author Arundhati Roy, "that the U.S. military presence in the Persian Gulf has little to do with its concern for human rights and almost entirely to do with its strategic interest in oil."

She documents how Unocal has been negotiating for years with the Taliban for permission to construct a pipeline through Afghanistan to Pakistan and out to the Arabian Sea. "In 1997, a delegation of Taliban mullahs traveled to America and even met with State Department officials in Washington and later with Unocal executives in Houston. At that time, the Taliban's taste for public executions and its treatment of Afghan women were not made out to be the crimes against humanity they are now. Over the next months, pressure from hundreds of outraged American feminist groups was brought to bear on the Clinton administration. Fortunately, they managed to scuttle the deal. But now comes the U.S. oil industry's big chance.

"In America," she continues, "the arms industry, the oil industry and the major media networks—indeed, U.S. foreign policy—are all controlled by the same business combines. It would be foolish to expect this talk of guns

90

and oil and defense deals to get any real play in the media. In any case, to a distraught, confused people whose pride has just been wounded, whose loved ones have been tragically killed, the inanities about the 'Clash of Civilizations" and the 'Good versus Evil' discourse home in unerringly.

"They are cynically doled out by government spokesmen like a daily dose of vitamins or anti-depressants. Regular medication ensures that mainland America continues to remain the enigma it has always been—a curiously insular people administered by a pathologically meddlesome, promiscuous government."

*

The strange and sad thing is, when the citizen analyzes American foreign policy and all our twists and turns in and out of wars, one comes to the realization that it's all *déjà vu*. History has seen these same manipulations over and over again.

In the 17th century, Shakespeare's Henry IV advises his son: "The best way to govern, young Harry, is to busy their giddy minds with foreign quarrels."

In the 20th century, historian Arnold Toynbee warns: "Military expansion is normally a result of militarism, which in itself is a symptom of decline."

So what else is new?

Maybe, God willing, that you and I and enough Americans demand a new way.

Princeton University, December 7ᵗʰ, 1941: Two of my closest college friends and I are in our dormitory room, drinking beer and listening to the radio crackle out the first news from Pearl Harbor. We're stunned, angered, excited. For three years we've been marching around together in Military Science, learning how to field strip French 75's from World War I. Totally boring stuff, but now it's real!

"Don't get too carried away," says Legs, the red-headed athlete. "This whole thing could be a phony, you know."

"Aw, come on," says Coach, the clown. "Those Japs weren't up in Hawaii to go surfing. And Hitler, too, that goofy Katzenjammer Kid will start attacking us tomorrow, you watch."

"Let him!" cries Legs. "We'll come down on all the buggers with both feet, six months maybe they'll go belly up, quit, declare Armistice. And the hell of it is, boys," he takes a long suck of his beer, "we'll still be in training. We'll miss the whole show."

Less than a year later, Coach is blown off a destroyer near Guadalcanal. He tries to swim free though depth charges exploding in the water. At daybreak, other sailors fish him out. The explosions have crushed him. He dies in their arms.

Legs is a hero, fights at Guam, decorated, becomes a General's aide. On Leyte, protecting his general, he walks a jungle road to search out snipers. One that he hasn't found shoots him through the head.

DIGGING OUT THE TRUTH: 2

Why War?

"It is fortunate that war is hell, or men would love it too much."

So said General William Tecumseh Sherman. But despite his admonition, we do love it. I know I did. I was fascinated by it. And now in the roar of war following 9/11, all of us are being subjected to killing day after day, stunned, deafened by TV's glorification of our magnificent violence. Our triumph of good over evil. Earth-shaking explosions, screaming jets, Strangelovian gleaming death tools, computerized carnage. It's the most stupendous, seductive fantasy that can entrap us, because it appeals to our primitive reflexes in our lowest levels of consciousness.

How can we resist it? How can we arm ourselves against it? To see through its massive magnetism? Because if we don't learn how to, and very soon, we may well be rushed into a spreading, senseless conflagration that could possibly engulf the world.

Perhaps one way to start de-fanging the gods of war is to expose the appeals that it makes to us. The myths we're being sold as just cause for our going off to fight.

One of the most provocative appeals is patriotism. Who doesn't want to love their country? Who isn't proud of it? In my own case, I thrilled at it. I longed to march in the company of heroes, never realizing where the march might lead me.

Gettysburg, PA, 1935: I'm 13, my brother, Bill, 15. In the April sun, we walk the green hills of the first battleground we've ever seen. We crawl into the grey rocks of Devil's Den, the snipers nest. We stride up the bloody hill of Pickett's noble charge. In an old frame house that peddles curios, we buy fistfuls of flattened minie balls and grooved horrific rifle slugs, bigger than our thumbs, imagining that they've blown six inch holes in Rebel bellies. In love with war. How can a young man not be?

We've been raised on it, our father flying a Curtiss Jenny in the First One, our uncle dropping bombs on

Huns in France, in a squadron commanded by a pudgy Italian, Fiorello LaGuardia. We play lead soldiers by the hour, we fight bike wars with rubber band machine guns on our handlebars. My uncle sings his squadron songs from France: "If he can fight like he can love, oh what a soldier boy he'll be...If he's half as good in a trench as he is in the park on bench...I know he'll be a hero when he's Over There, because he's such a bear in every Morris chair..."

Love and war, will it ever be ours?

From Gettysburg to Washington, stand in the shadowy Lincoln Memorial, stare up at the awesome man, the sadness in his face. Did he weep at Gettysburg that day he hallowed the dark and bloody ground? And then to Mount Vernon, the musty old rooms, Washington clacking his wooden teeth as he gives counsel to the young men who were building our nation. Black scrolled words leaping off the parchment of the Constitution. Jefferson, Madison, Hamilton, Jay, how did they create such a sacred document? How could they have had the vision to so change the world and set mankind free? Their average age was only 34!

Greatest nation on the face of the earth. God, the pride we feel, to be Americans!

A second tantalizing appeal of war is the promised romance and adventure in it. As the troops used to sing in World War I, "How you gonna keep 'em down on the farm after they've seen Paree?" War offers one an escape to a whole new world we didn't know was out there—a Paree that once we'd seen, made us long to go back home as quick as we could.

Bougainville, Solomon Islands, Christmas, 1943: I'm a 2ⁿᵈ Lieutenant in a Marine Corps transport squadron, Bill is a Major, commanding a battalion of armored artillery, training in England for the inevitable D-Day.

On this Christmas Eve, navigating our flight, I'm lost over Bougainville. Heavy blinding rain, soaking through the window seals of the cockpit. We've been in storm for hours, can't find the landmass which is as big as Long

Island. Ten days earlier, in the first flight of transports to reach the just opened Torokina strip, we had fighter escort, but now in the turbulence and rain, the fighters have abandoned us. Can't fly weather in single engine planes. We roar lower, away from the volcanic peaks of the island, break out into buffeting rain squalls. We're fifty feet over the Boungainville beach, don't know which way to turn. Head north, we could run into the Japanese fighter bases at Buka Passage. Head south, we could blunder over their strips in the Shortland islands. Torokina, our Marine beachhead, is only a tiny perimeter at Empress Augusta Bay. It's a bite we've taken out of the enemy, maybe three miles deep in jungle and ridges and one mile wide.

Our radio rattles with static: shout of an American pilot, blast of wing guns, then a raucous taunt from a Japanese. "Babu Rusu eat shit!" They think Babe Ruth is our god. Marine Corsairs are tangling with a flock of Zeroes over the fortress of Rabaul, a hundred miles west of us. "I flamed that sonofabitch!" an American cries. "Mark him down until he splashes!!"

We wheel south into a sharp bank, roar across the sodden beach and around a jungled point. Below us, people! A file, running in the rain, pot helmets, mustard colored uniforms, long sticks in their hands. Guns? Their faces whip up to us, only a few feet above them. They begin to scatter. The pilot beside me pushes back his baseball cap. "Goddamn," he breathes, "those were Japs!"

A few moments later, guns flash in the clouds. Marine artillery at Torokina. We slice in from the sea and rattle down on the steel Marston mat. Something blows, swerves the plane. A shell on the strip? When we park and shut down, we laugh at our jumpiness. All we blew was a tire. And to me, it's the best luck yet. We'll be grounded here until a new tire can be flown up from Guadalcanal. I'll get to see some real war now.

*

"The people want peace so much, one of these days governments are going to have to get our of their way and give it to them."

Dwight Eisenhower, 1950

"'You must understand that Americans are a warrior culture,' Senator Daniel Patrick Moynihan told a group of Arab leaders one month into the Middle East crisis. He said this proudly, and he may, without thinking through the ugly implications, have told the truth. In many ways, in outlook and behavior, the U.S. has begun to act like a primitive warrior culture."

Time magazine, 1990

*

In the wake of 9/11, we've been drenched with the Manichean notion that our enemies are Evil. Now this is certainly not new. In the last terrorist attack on U.S. soil, when Pancho Villa's army of *dorados* struck Columbus,

New Mexico in 1916, we reacted with the same horror response that gripped us after 9/11. Who was this beast? Put a face on him, a name we could hate.

Fortunately, our old Indian fighting chief of staff, General Hugh Scott, didn't quite buy it. He thundered, "Are we to go to war against one man? Folly! I won't send troops into such a wild goose chase!"

Eventually he was overruled, and we launched a "Punitive Expedition" against Villa and his terrorists. We fumbled around for over a year in the desert, never caught the symbol of evil—instead made Villa a hero to his people—infuriated the macho of both sides of the Mexican revolution, and in the end barely avoided war with all of Mexico. Finally we declared, not victory, but a humiliating draw. Our troops trudged home and began to ready themselves for the next and real war we knew we'd be fighting soon enough. Take down the next demon, the Kaiser and his Germany.

After 9/11, we reacted the same way, declared war on one man, the evil binLaden, did the necessary chasing around deserts and mountains and to date haven't found him. In fact, President Bush now says he's "irrelevant."

E.g. forget *that* evil one, broaden the war so we can rush on and find more to replace him.

The trouble with the "evil" concept is that whereas we may despise the face we're chasing, we find it hard to admit that our war of vengeance usually ends up putting the same evil face on us. In the mayhem of war, both sides descend into the same pit of man's inhumanity to man.

Bougainville, Christmas Eve, 1943: I'm in a mess tent near the airstrip, maybe thirty of us there, wooden benches, powdered eggs and dehydrated potatoes slopped on our tin plates. Outside, endless dark rain pattering the giant jungle trees. Then a strange whooping sound, far off. Is it coming closer? Somebody says, "Jungle parrot, they always squeal..."

A crash, a shatter. The wooden food locker at the end of the mess tent disintegrates. "Air raid!" somebody cries. Another: "That was no bomb. Damn artillery shell that didn't go off. Nip field gun up on the ridge. Their ammo is wet!"

We're all flyers here, not supposed to get shelled. We stumble out of the tent into slit trenches. Pitch dark now, tracers streaking the sky. Somebody shooting at something, nobody knows what. Half tracks filled with Marines are groaning past us, jeeps bogging down in the mud. No roads here, just endless mud, confusion. We're tripping over each other in the darkness. A friend I've known at Pensacola grabs me and leads me to the tent camp of his Corsair squadron. No lights anywhere. We think the shelling is over. Some of the Corsair boys break out a bottle of Three Feathers whiskey. Others snap on a flashlight and begin a poker game under a blanket.

Momentary. Again, the jungle comes alive, roars of artillery, nobody knows whose. Rattle of machine guns. Screams: "They're infiltrating! They're over here!" More blasting reports, hundred foot tall jungle trees hit by shells and crashing down. A groan: "You trigger happy assholes! Knock it off, you're shooting at Marines!"

Dark shapes running past us in the night, tripping, splatting cursing in the mud. We're in slit trenches again, shivering, stagnant water up to our bellies. The man next to me is doubled over with dysentery, can't hold it. I have my service.38 out, flailing it at mosquitoes. I'm coughing, whining clouds of them. A flash close by in the jungle. Shoot at it? Shoot who? I can't see. Machine guns, BAR's chatter their rounds through the trees above me, slicing down more branches. I scrunch deeper into the trench and press my face against the wet mud of the protecting side. It goes on for hours. Infiltration, false alarm? Nobody knows, just more screaming roaring in the night.

About three a.m., somebody must have sorted it out. The jungle goes quiet. We slog back into our tent. The fighter boys have only an hour left before they go up again over Rabaul. Drain the Three Feathers, last swig. The poker cards are floating in the flooded tent. I hear a sound at the entrance, a bare-legged man in a poncho moves past me. He's a soldier, rain dripping off his Army helmet liner. Bearded, his face yellowed with atabrine, his eyes dart around us. He giggles, "Got somethin', you guys." He lifts the poncho and takes out a wooden match box. It's wrapped in rubber bands which he peels off. "Gimme twenty bucks, hunh?" Somebody shines a flashlight. In the box are five Japanese teeth, the gold in them glinting. "Dug 'em out with a bayonet."

The flashlight snaps off. Wearily, one of the pilot murmurs, "Beat it, dogface. This is officers country." The man replaces each rubber band around his treasure and sloshes out into the darkness.

Christmas Day, I go into the jungle with a Marine wire-laying patrol. We reach the crest of a ridge, the front lines, small arms fire pinging in the valley just beyond us. The Marine Raiders holding the ridge don't seem to hear it. Bearded, half-naked, some are sitting in the mud munching soggy K-rations, others have hunkered into the cavernous trunks of giant jungle trees. They crowd around me, stranger, fly boy. "How's Notre Dame doin'?" "When you zoomies gonna bring us our fuckin' mail, hey? Been six weeks now." I don't have any answers, just *thank God I'm not one of these poor bastards, living like animals in trees.*

The next morning, we get our new tire and start loading wounded Marines for the flight back to Guadalcanal. The crewchief and a Navy corpsman strap in a half dozen litter cases. They're ashen-faced, plasma bottles dangling above them. Then there's commotion at the hatch of the plane. Three Marines are wrestling down a massive, screaming Fijian. He's a scout from the famous Fiji Patrol that's been operating behind the Japanese lines. They use knives, not guns, kill the enemy one by one. Wooly-headed, bones in his ear lobes, this brave man has gone mad. We all fight him down onto a litter, use our belts to tie him even tighter. He's writhing and moaning so wildly the corpsman can barely jab morphine into his arm.

Just as I'm starting back to the flight deck, a Marine officer shouts from the rear hatch. He's shoving ahead of him three tiny figures in ill-fitting U.S. dungarees. Their black heads are shaved, their eyes sullen, terrified. I can't believe it. Japanese girls! Their ages are unreadable but they've got to be still in their teens. "Nip comfort women," says the officer. "Intelligence wants 'em down at the Canal."

As he straps them into the bucket seats, one of the wounded Marines lifts up from his litter. "Fuckin' whores, slice 'em from you know what right up to the neck, toss 'em in the drink. That's what I'd do."

Gently, the officer pushes him back down on the litter. "Knock it off, Mac. Your war is over."

We trundle out on the strip into takeoff position. Two Corsairs pull in behind us. Just as the pilot pushes up the throttles, I see it coming, cry: "Hold it!" From the other end of the strip, a flash of white against the jungle: a New Zealand Ventura bomber has lost one engine. It's feathered, smoking. Wobbling, veering, the plane is making a downwind landing, rushing directly at us. No room on the mat to turn around, can't get out of his way. He hits, bounces, and then miraculously, wheels off into the mud and rocks to a stop, yards from us.

"Holy shit," breathes the pilot. "there's a Christmas present for you." Hand trembling, he guns the throttles and we roar off into the rain. One down, how many more to go?

*

"Where there is no love of man, no love of life, then make all the laws you want, all the edicts and treaties—as long as you see your fellow man as a being essentially to be feared, mistrusted, hated and destroyed, there cannot be peace on earth."

Thomas Merton

*

The last compelling appeal of war is that it gives us a chance to show our courage. Raw guts. Were we supposed to take the insult of 9/11 lying down? No way! Sic 'em, get 'em! We're men enough, aren't we? Balls!

What a provocative lure it is. Noble, too. Sacrifice your life for someone else. A greater cause.

And yes, there were heroes, incredibly brave ones. But there is also the morning after, for those still around to see it. Almost invariably—and I've talked to hundreds of combat veterans—their lips tighten and they ask quietly: what had it all been for? That's what they don't tell us in the glory of TV war. You have to see it yourself, hear the silence of the dead once more, before you can resist the siren song of war.

Pelelieu Island, October 12, 1944: I walk with General Geiger toward Bloody Nose Ridge, jagged, fierce moonscape of coral, rising hundreds of feet high, all vegetation blasted away. It's like the shattered spine of a dead white beast, lying face down in the mangrove swamps of a tiny island. For years the Japanese have been waiting for us to attack it, digging a slaughterhouse network of tunnels and caves. Geiger and Admiral Halsey know this. They plead with headquarters that Pelelieu's original mission of protecting MacArthur's beachhead in the Philippines is now unnecessary. He's already landed at Leyte. Washington's answer: too late, operation scheduled, cannot be called off.

So here in the smoke and roar of battle, Corsairs are screaming down on the Ridge, blasting napalm into the myriad caves of the Japanese. Suffocate them, blast them out with 155mm Long Tom artillery shells. But day and night they still hold on, rats in holes, some with steel doors, most constructed ingeniously with 90 degree turns in the tunnels so that enemy fire can't reach them. On a single slope of the Ridge, no bigger than a football field, one of Geiger's colonels has already lost a thousand men.

We're close enough to the Ridge that sniper fire is hissing past us. Geiger, like me, is unarmed. As we near a wrecked Japanese fortification, a Marine Master Sergeant motions at us to get down. He's Geiger's longtime bodyguard, a hard-faced Texan with a pair of Colt.45 frontier type revolvers in his hands. He nods at the wrecked building, Sniper in there. Take cover, General.

Geiger has told me once: "I've been in so much combat, I figure I've used up all my chances." Instead of taking cover, he turns his back and takes a leak. The Texan and other Marines blast out the sniper. We move on a hundred yards or so, pausing by a group of dug-in Marines. A mortar position. As Geiger watches, they chuff off several rounds, bursting on the lower slopes of the Ridge. A Colonel, an old-time China Marine comrade of Geiger's strides towards us.

A flat, greenish crack. Somebody shouts, others running, ducking. The Colonel is down, writhing in pain. A Japanese knee mortar shell has exploded among us, the fragments striking him in the kidneys. He dies that night.

I follow Geiger up onto the slope of the ridge. Above us, only hundreds of yards away, I stare at the dark eye holes of caves. We know the enemy is in there, know they watch us. Geiger strides over to a long coral ditch where dozens of Marine riflemen are crouching. I'm stunned. These are kids...sixteen, seventeen, I don't know how old, but they're all that's left now of the proud First Marine Division. Replacements for the veterans who have died at Guadalcanal, Cape Gloucester and now this. Their camoflauged helmets seem bigger than they are. Heavy with bandoliers of ammunition and grenades, some of the riflemen are tense, white-faced, first time they're being shot at. But others are tough kids, Hell's Kitchen types, Italians, Irish, Poles, maybe New York, Boston, Philly, Chicago.

Geiger kneels beside them. They're down protected by the coral trench, but he's on top, wearing khakis, his two stars and wings. The Japanese above us have to see him. I want to curse his folly—and then love him for it.

Showing the flag, giving courage to these kids of his. He goes from man to man. He has no small talk. It's not his way. Just a gruff pat on the shoulder, a thumbs up. The kids smile, some try to salute but he waves them off. Then he turns and looks at the platoon commanders who are spread out along the trench. They wear no insignia that the Japanese can target on. Just ragged, coral dusted dungarees.

A Captain nods at Geiger. Then he scrambles out of the trench and blows a whistle. Other whistles sound all along the line. The Marine kids go, half bent over, running up the slope of the Ridge. They scatter, take cover among blasted coral rocks. Some are firing at shapes we can't see. Demolition charges are hurled into the caves. They run higher into chattering fire increasing every minute.

The Ridge top is hundreds of feet above them. The objective. Get there, hold it. They're far from us now, tiny black specks clawing their way up through the coral. There are no cries, no human sound above the roar of war. I see one speck sit down. Others crowd around him. Whitish blast of a shell. They're gone, black objects scattered in the coral. None get up. The long line curls and works higher on the left side of the Ridge. Now many are falling, but more go on, more are nearing the top.

When they reach it—and they reach it day after day—it's over a hundred degrees up there. Searing sun, no shade, no water. Ammo low, too much shot up on the slope. Nobody reinforces them. Not enough left. By the time the sun flames away and the Ridge falls in shadow, they can't hold. Have to fight their way back down, carrying if they can the corpses of their buddies.

For a worthless, strategically unnecessary hunk of coral, five miles long by three miles wide, 9,172 kids like these will be wounded or dead, and with them, 11,000 Japanese, fighting almost to the last man.

In 1973, I have to see Pelelieu one last time. Quiet now, only the shrieks of parrots in the jungle canopy. The Ridge is healed, greened, a forest of towering barringtonia trees. In the ghostly caves, I find Japanese helmets, tins of fish, unfired ammunition and mortar shells. Beside them, American first aid kits, scattered and open with bandages still in them. A faint breeze comes up from the Pacific and moans through a Japanese

Nambu machine gun, its cartridge belt still in the breech, ready to fire.

Who died here, who remembered? A Palauan native tells me I'm only the third American ever to come back. I stumble out of the cave into the sunlight, tears in my eyes.

*

"War itself, as a means of settling differences between great powers will have to in some way be ruled out, and with it will have to be dismantled the greater part of the vast military establishments now maintained. It is the ingrained habits and assumptions of men, and above all, of men in government which alone can guarantee any enduring state of peaceful relations among nations."

George Kennan, former U.S. Ambassador to the Soviet Union; chief planner of U.S. Cold War policy.

*

Take the appeals apart one by one, live them again in the horror of the 9/11 war, but in the end, each of us is left with the unanswered question. Why war at all? Is it the only way we know now to solve the differences between us?

Isn't it finally time to resist the propaganda and move on to the new?

New York, September 11ᵗʰ, 2001: The twin towers roaring down, people leaping to their deaths. The Pentagon on fire. The anthrax letters, the deadly wriggling spores. Osama Bin Laden framed in a Christ-like hood, firing an automatic weapon. Ambulances screaming, dead carried away in caskets draped with American flags. Armed soldiers and sniffer dogs in airports. Bombs? Smallpox next? Nuclear weapons? Highest alerts from Washington: expect next terrorist attack within three days, within one day, within...When? President Bush: "A 50 year war against Evil."

<u>"Big Brother, in order to control the population, knew that it was necessary for the people to always believe they were in a state of siege, that the enemy was getting closer and closer and that the war would take a very long time."</u>

George Orwell, England, 1930

"The people can always be brought to do the bidding of the leaders. That is easy. All you do is tell them they are being attacked, and denounce the pacifists for lack of patriotism."

Hermann Goering, Nazi Germany, 1941

RESISTING WAR PROPAGANDA: 1

"Evil Empire." "Leave it Colored Red."

In 1946, when Harry Truman was about to launch the Cold War, veteran Senator Arthur Vandenberg of Michigan warned him: "You're going to have to scare hell out of the American people to make them spend all that money in peacetime."

Minneapolis, 1947: I'm a green reporter on the Star. *My deskmate, an old news veteran, thrusts me a teletype just off the wire from Washington. It's labeled Department of Defense. "Russian Bomber Sighted Over Alaska." My deskmate smiles. "Wake up, kid, don't you get it?"*

"Get what?"

"They've got a fight over military appropriations coming up in Congress. There's opposition so they've got to scare the dummies into giving them more dough. Next week, count on it, they'll probably surface a Russian sub off California."

I think: you cynical bastard, you sit out four years of war behind your desk and now you're the expert. "Aw, come on," I say, "our government doesn't work that way."

I was reacting like any veteran, back from World War II, star spangles in our eyes, full of pride in our nation and hope for the future. It was all love and kids and career. I'd never been a political person. The last thing I wanted to think about was more war, least of all to suspect that our government was manipulating my patriotism with fear.

I wasn't alert enough to question why our old War and Navy Departments had suddenly been melded into something called Department of Defense. It never occurred to me that war propaganda had now become language. While we dozed in our peace dreams, our managers in Washington had already hatched their Grand Area scheme. It was to expand and protect our worldwide markets. Under the guise of making the world safe for democracy, it was actually to make our corporations safe to sell and profit by our ever-more bounteous gross national product. We were on the road.

In Oliver Stone's movie <u>JFK</u>, there's a scene where a Mr. X sits down on a park bench and gives Kevin Costner chapter and verse on who pulled off the plot to kill the President.

The real Mr. X is a man named Fletcher Prouty. He's now a veteran defense analyst. He'd taught at Yale and served in the government. But several days after V-J day in 1945, Prouty was an Air Corps colonel flying a transport into Okinawa. He happened to stroll down to the docks and saw lines of tanks, trucks, artillery being loaded aboard Navy vessels. He assumed the stuff was being returned to the States, but the Navy dockmaster shook his head. It was being shipped to Korea and Indo-China, which was not even being called Vietnam at the time. Prouty was astounded. Why to those places? We weren't fighting there. The war was over, wasn't it? He got no answer. The Navy dockmaster didn't know either, and was just following orders.

Washington was already setting up our "defense" of Korea and Indo-China. Had the public known, somebody might have tried to stop it. But in 1945, the foreign policy elites knew they couldn't sell their Grand Area scheme by tipping their mitt that the result of protecting American corporate markets would inevitably lead to future wars. They didn't dare admit the possibility of war to a nation basking in peace. How about Defense, though? Didn't that connote security and guarantee us comfort in our lives? Pull up the covers and go to sleep. Nobody could argue if we were "defending" against enemies attacking us.

Dwight Eisenhower knew what was happening when in his final speech as President, he warned the nation about the incredible power of the military-industrial complex. We were launching the Cold War to bring our "freedom" (e.g. a free market in which we could sell our goods) to peoples we regarded as backward, 3rd World, and so we divided humanity into Us vs Them. To get the public to buy it, use the propaganda of war. Demon-making. We had to paint the Russians, the Soviets, the commies as massive evil empire threats to our lives, liberties and pursuits of happiness. To scare hell out of American citizens, as Arthur Vandenberg said, was the surest way to get Congress to pass gargantuan defense appropriations.

Minneapolis, 1948: My tough old city editor sends me out to interview the first dreaded communist I've ever met. Gerhard Eisler, an East German provocateur and, I assumed, obviously spying here for some occult reason in safe old Minneapolis. "I don't want that sonofabitch saying we don't have a free press!" the city editor rasps. "Give him four paragraphs." I find the bespectacled little guy in a crummy hotel. He doesn't seem all that evil, in fact insipid, but he does have a motor mouth, spewing out the party line. How in hell, I think, can anybody believe that crap? I give him two paragraphs.

Chicago, Ill. 1951: a fellow reporter and I quit the dreary newsroom. Leap into TV, form a production company with $15,000. High burn rate, in three years we're broke. Tail between my legs, haul Teddy and our three boys back to Lake Forest where I grew up. My father keeps saying, "Get on somebody's payroll."

Well, what about going back into the Marine Corps? We're into Korea now, evil really closing in. Before an answer comes back from the Corps, a college friend hits me up to join CIA. Secret bios and clandestine phone calls, beginning to get spooky. By now, I'm writing TV commercials for a major advertising agency, more money than I could ever be worth and hating every minute of it. Sitting in endless meetings deciding whether our client's refrigerator should open in my commercial with a "whoosh" or a "whaash."

Old Corps and college friends are getting shot at in Korea, and I'm doing this idiocy? I bag CIA and the ad game and go back to freelancing. A priest tells me about a Czech girl, actually a countess, who made a perilous escape through the Iron Curtain. I interview her, poor thing is so scared and tongue-tied I have to hide my tape recorder under the sofa. But with war everywhere, her story fires me up. It runs in three installments, Chicago Tribune Syndicate.

Funny thing, an acquaintance from Minneapolis calls and asks me to write a one reeler anti-commie picture. He's a high level corporate executive, and I wonder why he's mixed up with something called Radio Free Europe. Only later I find out that CIA is shilling for public support to beam freedom's message behind the Iron Curtain, and is picking up the check for most of it.

Anyway, I jump at it, title the film <u>The Bell.</u> (I can't remember now if it was our Liberty Bell or some bullet-pranged one our GI's had liberated from the Russians when they were stealing East Germany.) I write in a part for General Lucius Clay, hero of the Berlin Airlift and all the nastiness going on over there. Henry Fonda does the narration, and when President Eisenhower hears about it, he wants to be in it too. (I'd already filmed him once for <u>Cinerama.</u> During that shoot, he approached me in his grinning, easy way and asked if I'd hold up things until Mamie could go back into the White House and put on her new pink hat.}

Los Angeles, CA, 1952: Maybe <u>The Bell</u> has rung the cash register at Radio Free Europe, because now they call again, want a second one-reeler. Pull out the stops on this one, get a stand up actor, an appealing American figure not only to do the voice over but appear in person. Sell it.

By now I know a few actors, in fact I'm working for Jack Webb, Sergeant Friday of <u>Dragnet</u>. But Jack, an orphan, grew up in a police station. Too coppish. What about Peter Lawford who'd married JFK's sister, Pat Kennedy. Cheery Peter, too Britishy, also a Demo. He wouldn't be right for this mainly Republican show. Who, though?

Clipping in the paper. My God, Nancy Davis has just married a B picture actor, Ronald Reagan! I'd grown up with Nancy in Chicago, same Latin schools, roller-skated the Gold Coast together, waltzed primly at dancing school. A great girl, Nancy. I call her and within an hour, I'm out at their house in Pacific Palisades. Ronnie strides in, gives me that genial handshake. Hell, yes, he'll be honored to do the picture. He's been fighting commies in the film industry.

So I put in some jack-booted commissars, really evil guys. Our exile hero has heard Radio Free Europe. Its message of freedom gives him the guts to run through the Iron Curtain and come down on our side. The Big Truth, I call it.

We win a Freedom Foundation Award. When I tell Ronnie, he grins and says, "Your words did it."

What they did, unbeknownst to any of us, was to bring the Reagans and ourselves together in our common determination to defeat the Evil Empire.

Beverly Hills, CA, November 1964: a day after the election that Barry Goldwater has just lost to Lyndon Johnson, Nancy Reagan, sounding tired and distraught, calls and asks if she and Ronnie can come over for dinner. When they get there, we go into the study and have a drink. Ronnie drops the bombshell. That morning, the Republican power group in California has

*asked him to run for governor. "I told them," he says, "I
don't want to savage other candidates. I won't be party
to political fights. But if they could clear the way for
me..." he shakes his head uncertainly. "All these years
I've been making speeches about what we ought to do in
this country, get out of the mess we're in. Now they've
dropped the ball in my court. Don't I have to pick it up
and run with it? What do you think, Otis?"*

"Hell yes," I say. "You pretty much have to."

*After dinner, Nancy is in our bedroom with Teddy,
sitting on our bed with tears rolling down her cheeks.
"Ronnie and I have such a wonderful life together. We
love each other so much. After these last terrible weeks of
the campaign, all I can think is: why? Why do we need
to wreck what we have and get the garbage of politics
dumped all over us?"*

*Hours later, they go home and I turn to Teddy.
"Damn, they're such decent people—a humble, kindly
guy like Ronnie—put him into the political jungle, those
gorillas will tear him to bits..."*

*

War propaganda is so effective because it's not off the wall. It has to have just enough elements of truth in it to make you believe it. Take the Evil Empire. It was all of that. The Soviet Union was a brutal, suffering place. The Russians were dangerous. They had nuclear weapons and immense armed forces. But they had also lost 22 million of their people in World War II. Despite their threats about burying us, they were a wasted, basically primitive nation leading more from bluff than strength. They dreaded the horrors of another war, and lived in fear that we would wreak one upon them. Justifiably so, because our containment policy had encircled them in a ring of steel.

Americans went along with the Cold War for two important reasons: our politicians needed it, and we needed it in the pocketbook. Our managers learned that if they terrified us enough they could manipulate the Soviet demon to rise and fall more or less on cue. Economy slipping, facing a recession? An administration in trouble in the polls? Snatch the ogre out of the closet, dust him off, and if a politician ran for re-election on hard-line anti-communism, he was practically a slam dunk to win. Moreover, because of the "war," he had a fistful of defense goodies to give away.

The B-1 bomber, for example, was jiggered through Congress by the simple expedient of having at least one of its myriad parts manufactured in each congressional district of the nation. As for us nobodies, ordinary citizens, not only were we scared to death but we bought into the Cold War myth because it created jobs, a horn of plenty pumping out our good life, and thus we accepted the crushing debt and reduced freedoms of a warfare state. Bomb shelters at first, then school kids being drilled to hide under their desks lest the **Big One** hit. And finally, pock-marking our land with forts, airbases and missile sites.

Why did the Cold War continue for so long? Another more tragic reason has been advanced.

During World War II especially, but throughout their long history, the Jewish people have been victims of terrible atrocities. When the Iron Curtain clanged down,

Jews by the hundreds of thousands were trapped behind it. To them, though Hitler was a murderous anti-Semite, Stalin's Russia was no better. For centuries, Russian rulers had been violently anti-Semitic. They had driven Jews out of their sacred capital and kept them geographically "beyond the pale." Having just survived the ravages of Hitler, the Jews were now out of the frying pan and into the Soviet fire. Understandably, they developed a violent hatred for the Soviets and Russian concentration camp communism.

Nothing would please them more than to have the Soviet Union destroyed, especially so because the communists were already supporting neighboring Arab countries who had vowed to wipe out the fledgling state of Israel. Because the U.S. was the only nation with the power to defeat the Soviets, Israelis backed the Cold War passionately, and used their considerable influence in Washington to keep it aflame.

While the Cold War was still raging, I was invited to London for a seminar of U.S. military and industrial leaders. I was supposed to give a brief talk, asking the question: was the Cold War really necessary, and how could we get beyond it? I never got off the bench, too many other speakers with more important things to say. The conference room sparkled with generals, cabinet secretaries and CEO's of some of our largest corporations. The Pentagon had prepared a costly doomsday book, showing in living color the arsenal of dreadful Soviet weaponry. Terror was being sold here.

I spent some time talking to a bright young fellow who was one of Ronnie Reagan's national security advisors. A few moments later, the wife of one of our top State Department people approached me. "Don't believe what that guy tells you," she said. "He's an Israeli first and an American second."

Shortly thereafter, a friend who was CEO of a major corporation, began doing business with the Soviet Union. When word leaked out about it, Israeli-supporters in the U.S. retaliated against him. He received a thick file of angry letters. Distributors refused to carry his company's products. Garbage was heaped in front of his factories. There were even threats on his life because he had dared to say the Soviets were human beings after all, businessmen like ourselves, and we had better start trusting them and healing our differences.

When the Cold War finally ended, a Russian general said sardonically: "We have taken your enemy from you. What will you Americans do now to run your country?"

I didn't know any of that then. Having swallowed the manipulated patriotism of the Cold War, I kept on trying to fight it in words, wake people up. I wrote a full length documentary feature for Paramount. <u>Russia and the West</u>, based on Ambassador George Kennan's book. The producer jiggered it around into violent anti-commie propaganda—Kennan's book was reasonable, and anything but this. Then the producer drank himself to death. The studio never released the film, fearing the theaters would be stink-bombed by commie agitators.

A crazy time. I did a novel, <u>Good Friday 1963,</u> a plea that citizens get in and start exercising responsibility, put pressure on the government so that we could end the interminable fear and violence of the Cold War. The book struck a chord, went through several editions. I did a lot of speaking about it, women's groups usually. Everybody seemed to want to know what they could do to get the country back on track. Then JFK was killed. All of us went into shock. Where now?

I found out.

Beverly Hills, CA, October, 1963 The CIA, under orders from the Kennedy administration, has just destroyed the Diem government in Vietnam. Because of my novel, a French intelligence agent comes to see me. An ex-communist, she had helped author the NATO manual on psycho-political warfare. She'd also been with President Diem and Counselor Nhu the night before they were murdered, a by-product of the botched CIA coup. She tells me the U.S. has now created a vacuum of power that we can only fill by plunging American troops into a massive land war in Asia. "How do I know?" she says. "Because exactly the same thing happened to us in France. You are involving yourselves in an unwinnable civil war. Our war was settled not on the battlefield but by riots in France. Yours will end in riots on the streets of America."

I'm stunned. I call in friends to listen to her. At this point in 1963, the U.S. has only a few thousand military observers in Vietnam, but the French agent is talking in terms of armies. Obviously, we're being duped into a war nobody wants. The public has to be warned.

We think we can do it. Maybe a dozen of us are listening to her in the living room of our house in Beverly Hills. Some are journalists, a few ex-government with good Washington contacts. Ronnie and Nancy Reagan are there too. As a TV spokesman for General Electric, Ronnie has considerable visibility. Certainly between us we can muster up press coverage on such a shocking revelation. Immediately we begin calling our friends in the media. Their answer is always the same: Our story doesn't jibe with Washington's story.

For weeks, the Administration has been launching massive war propaganda, dramatizing why we have to become involved in Vietnam. We, now, are threatening to spike that lie. The result? We can't get a single line in a newspaper or a sound byte even on local TV. I'm so *enraged that I write a novel, <u>The Paper Bullet</u>, dramatizing how the American people have been patriotically manipulated to rush into war. By the time the book comes out, we have thousands of troops in Vietnam, launching the major land disaster the French agent has predicted.*

The rest is history. We plunged into an unwinnable civil war on the other side of the world because we had been propagandized to believe that the dominoes would fall and Asia would go communist. Fall they did, the only effect being that our communist enemies became capitalists on the war riches we'd left behind, and are now hiring corporate America to build them luxury hotels and golf courses. Diplomatic recognition comes next, a booming market in which to sell our products.

The U.S. lost no freedoms to evil empires. The loss was good kids who knew not why they were there. Forty-seven thousand Americans with their names on the black marble wall in Washington. Probably two million Vietnamese, unnamed but dead nonetheless. When it finally did end, a Marine General stood on the roof of our embassy in Saigon and watched the last of our defeated troops being evacuated by chopper. He asked sadly, "What has it all been for?"

When my novel finally leaks out, a state secret would have got more publicity. Reviewers don't want to believe that such pervasive war propaganda exists, let alone has the power to plunge us into actions deleterious to our nation. My agent and publishers beg me to get off the soapbox. Forget the Cold War, go back to boy-girl stories, or better yet Westerns, where the guy in the white hat always wins.

When you reach the point where war propaganda becomes repugnant to you—a voice contrary to your spirit—and each of us has to come to it in our own way—when you get into resisting it, your view of the world begins to change. You begin to see that the ancient cry of kill or be killed is being used as a propaganda tool. You begin to see that sharpening your own discernment is essential: that recognizing the myths of propaganda is the only way to go free. As the poet ee cummings wrote:" "To be nobody but yourself in a world that it is trying to turn you into everybody else is the hardest battle any human being can ever fight—and keep on fighting."

At that time, Barry Goldwater seemed to be our patriotic American white hope, to defeat seamy Lyndon B. Johnson, who was only dragging us deeper into the quagmire of Vietnam. I hurled myself into flacking for politics.

Beverly Hills, CA, October 1964. The Republican National Committee hires me to do a TV special for Goldwater's campaign. I title it CHOICE, the theme: there are two Americas out there, folks, LBJ's seamy and corrupt, Goldwater's clean and honest: choose which one you want. I persuade John Wayne to do an ending for the film, and bring in Raymond Massey as a homespun Abe Lincoln in Illinois narrator.

All downhill from there, into the dirty swamp of national politics. Clandestine meetings, memos from Washington slid into our pockets as if they contain secrets of the A-bomb. We hope to do a sequence of LBJ's cronies

Bobby Baker and Billy Sol Estes. Though they've both been testifying to Congress and are covered by thousands of feet of news footage, when we approach film libraries, not one foot of their testimony is available. The Administration has pulled it. We have to do the sequence with stills, all we can get.

We don't talk on phones, might be bugged, our identities be revealed. Then the real bomb goes off. One night, agents of the Democratic National Committee, a la Watergate, break into our secret studio and steal one of the prints. When it reaches Washington, a thunderclap of outrage. Herblock is doing daily lurid cartoons in the Washington Post, *exposing the perpetrators of this plot to vilify our President, columns filled with accusations of Republicans stooping to pornography. I'm hiding in a foxhole in my Beverly Hills house. If my right-wing conspirator name ever surfaces, curtains for any tenuous film career I might have.*

Duke Wayne comes down with the same dose of panic. He's on the phone, threatening me with legal action if I don't get him off the picture. I say, "But Duke, I read you the script. You approved it." No matter. Too much heat in the kitchen. Finally Barry Goldwater's advisors pull the picture. It's never shown. In a press conference the day after the election, reporters are given the one and only public glimpse of Choice. The New York Herald Tribune writes: "This was the finest campaign material Goldwater had. It was exactly what he'd been saying throughout the campaign. It should never have been cancelled."

Years later, the New York Sunday Times does a full page of text and scenes from the film, saying: "Choice changed political dialogue in America forever."

I thought that was my swansong in politics, but not quite yet.

Encino, CA, October, 1964: it's a week after Goldwater has ditched Choice, Duke Wayne calls me, apologetic, sorry about that. Now, he wants me to write his own TV special, give him a chance to show how the commies are stealing the world. He's scrawled some notes on a legal pad, I bust my butt to make a screenplay out of them in less than a week. The hurry is, Duke has me go over and see an unemployed politician named Dick Nixon. Actually, I know him slightly because as a Navy air base officer, he used to sign our flight manifests when we landed at Guadalcanal. Anyhow, Nixon is delighted to get involved and agrees to do a tag ending on the film.

Wayne, 'The Duke" is a guy you can't help but like. Real patriot, rough and tumble, too many times we've stayed up half the night, hearing him bellow out history and politics over more drinks than I need. Sometimes Pilar, his wife, gives up on him and goes home. We pack him off in the wee hours in a taxi.

Now we're into the last day of filming our TV special. Have to do it at Duke's house because he's wan and frail from a cancer operation. Can't take studio lights. We've hung a wall map over his fireplace, showing the nations the communists have stolen from us colored in red.

Wayne taps them on cue and rasps out his attack on our failed foreign policy. But in the middle of a take, I notice that Italy and France have suddenly blossomed out just as red as their communist neighbors. "On Mr. Wayne's orders," says the art director. "Duke," I plead, "you can't do that. Italy and France aren't communist!" He whirls. "Well, goddammit, if they're not, they're gonna be any day now! Leave it colored red!"

When Duke goes off to take a breather and smoke a cigar (which he's forbidden to do with his lung cancer), I sneak in the art director and have him spray paint Italy and France back to Freedom's Side. Duke never notices the change.

But something was changing in me, which was why, when the end finally came, it was like pushing forever against an iron door, and then miraculously having it burst open. I was sick of politics, war propaganda, and worse, being used by it. My spirit, however haltingly and painfully, was begging me to get beyond all this and be myself. Start writing what I truly believed.

In 1976, I did a piece in the <u>Wall Street Journal</u> about land takeovers in Mexico. Not really communists, just a bandit government at work. Ronnie liked it, called and asked me to put some of those thoughts into a campaign speech for him. (His first failed run at the Presidency.) By then I was thinking more about the human spirit than politics, so I wrote him what was really an idealistic appeal that we put our American soul back into our governing, titling it, unoriginally, <u>God Bless America.</u>

A few days later, I went down to the ranch mailbox and found a handwritten note from him in Pacific Palisades:

> "Dear Otis,
>
> Home to pick up clean laundry and your speech—please, my heart-felt thanks. Maybe I'll just keep it for Sunday mornings on the road when I can't get to church. I'm not joking Otis it's beautiful and will be of great value to me. Again, please accept my gratitude. I'll try to be deserving.
>
> Ron

To my knowledge, he never used a word of the speech.

I'd written a no-no, talking about soul. Though Ronnie was a church-goer and a believer, for a pragmatic politician, dedicated to doing/winning, the vapory being of soul had to be anathema. Soul smacked of religion, and no politician dared mix the two. Indeed, hadn't we pretty much burned out soul in generations of faithful churching that mixed up God with religion until we thought that the rotes of it were all we needed to find our spirit? Small wonder that so many of our youth abandoned religion entirely, and even the loyal believers were searching more and more for answers they weren't getting from the pulpit.

Then, a strange thing happened that seemed to draw us back together.

New York, November 21, 1986. Park Avenue apartment, eight or ten big men, movers and shakers in government, media and finance gathered here to watch Ronnie Reagan on TV.

In my long ago speech for Ronnie, I wrote a joke about a city feller asking a farmer for directions. When the farmer doesn't know where any road leads, the city feller finally explodes: "Then what the hell do you know?"

Farmer says, "I ain't lost."

But poor Ronnie is clearly lost in the fog, this night of November 21, 1986, in confusion, fumbling around trying to defend himself to the press for the Iran-Contra scandal. What did he know and when did he know it? His TV audience, including us in the apartment, are even more lost, as if suddenly we're in a place we don't want to be, and don't know how we'd got there.

I truly feel for him. Over the next weeks, the press is on him like a hound pack. There's even talk that he's so depressed now, he'll either be impeached or have to resign. On top of this, surgeons get to carving on his prostate. By Christmas night, I'm moved to drop him a quick note, saying, Look, you've had the world dump in on you. I only want to tell you and Nancy that you're good people, you've done many good things—in short, you're worthy human beings, far beyond this moment of political sound and fury.

A few days later, I'm at the kitchen sink at the ranch, cleaning some quail I've shot. When I pick up the phone, I've got feathers on my hands, and Ronnie and Nancy both at the other end. "I'm sitting here looking at the letter you wrote Nancy and me," Ronnie says, in a voice that is as tired and downcast as I've ever heard it. "I just want to tell you, Otis, how much it means to us."

We talk a long time, Ronnie, with Nancy chiming in, saying over and over that he did not know about the Iran-Contra deal. The press, and he named names, was trying to crucify him with it.

When we finally hang up, I'm torn to want to believe him—and yet the avalanche of accusations thundering over him makes me doubt myself. Who's right, who's wrong? Mostly it saddens me that he'd be so down in the bottom of the barrel that he has to reach out to somebody, to tell his story. An anybody. I'm not a donor, a party biggie, I can't do anything for him. Nothing but an old friend he could trust. Maybe that's enough...

All I could think then, and regret, was how far we'd drifted apart. I wasn't even a Republican anymore. I'd shot past liberal and out the far end to radical: one who digs out the roots. Again and again, in my letters to Ronnie and Nancy, I'd tried to encourage them to end the Cold War. End the war propaganda that was keeping the world frozen in fear.

I knew Ronnie was a good man, so kindly that he kept up a voluminous correspondence, hand-writing notes to hundreds of Americans, total strangers whom he felt obliged to help. Often he'd send them donations out of his own pocket. Yet on the other hand, this same man could seem oblivious to the "crimes of patriots" his administration was performing. Why would he not know what a secret arm of his government was doing in his name?

I was appalled by his determination to run up the largest military budget in history and the largest deficit. Bury the Soviets with dollars, this from a man who was a dedicated fiscal conservative. Days after his first election as California's governor, I watched him stand up in front of a group of his heaviest backers, tough, California businessmen, self-made millionaires. They growled protest when Ronnie said he was canceling the proposed governor's mansion and other bloated state programs. "I intend to govern," he said, "like I'm in there for one term only. Do what I believe is right and best for the state, not for my re-election."

Why the change? In my view, he was trapped in the system. He had to go along to get along—realizing it was the only way he could push his legislative program through Congress. It wasn't his nature to enjoy political in-fighting. Rather, he tried to detach himself, sometimes even dozing through meetings. He felt confident that he'd picked good men, gave them his trust that they would carry out his policies.

I suspect that it wasn't long before the foreign policy and military-industrial elites stepped into the vacuum. By appealing to his rock-ribbed Middle Western patriotism, they pretty much set their own agendas— convincing themselves that it was what he would want—

and then felt free to carry them out. Thus, they took advantage of a decent man who believed in the cavalry charging over the hill and saving the hero in the nick of time. Believed the American Movie Story, John Ford tying yellow ribbons on Monument Valley.

So the sharks came around him, federal blood in the water. I saw plenty of corporate defense suppliers circling Ronnie when we'd visit him at the White House. Some were so sleazy I wanted to hold onto my wallet. And others, I'm sure, gifted PR men, were playing on his heartstrings to let them go clean the commies out of Nicaragua before they attacked Disneyland. All evil, our enemies.

But not forever.

The White House, June, 1988. Twenty-four years after that day Duke Wayne tried to color it red, Ronnie and Nancy are standing with Teddy and me in the South Portico. They've just returned from their first epochal meeting with Gorbachev in Geneva. Ronnie grips me in his robust way, hugs Teddy and I hug Nancy like we're back again at dancing school. A photographer scurries in and takes our picture.

I think of all my letters over the years, begging Ronnie to see through the fraud of the Cold War and end it. So now that they're just back from the heart of darkness, I wonder what their reaction is going to be. I thank them for their courage in making this great leap toward peace.

Ronnie grins. "Listen, it wasn't hard to do. I've got to tell you, Otis, those Russians are wonderful people. Sure, they tried to bug us in the shower and everyplace else, we practically had to walk around naked to talk to each other, but that's just their suspicious way. They're great, we really enjoyed them." Nancy adds, "This window of opportunity Ronnie has opened has to stay open. We've got to keep this thing going, and change the way we think about Russia."

I gasp. Am I hearing right? Russians wonderful people? What happened to the Evil Empire? Korea, Cuban missile crisis, Berlin Airlift. Vietnam, Grenada, Nicaragua? Evil turned suddenly good? Then why all the treasure and the lives of Americans we've flung away, defending against it? I'm un-moored, even sickened.

All myth. We've died for a myth. The Russians are now, and ever have been, human beings, longing for spirit just as we.

When it's over and Teddy and I walk out on Pennsylvania Avenue, I could only whisper, "What a turn-around! Can you believe it?"

"Thank God," she says. Then even the roar of rush hour traffic seems quieter. We sit down in an outdoor restaurant, no need for words. Just sitting still, counting our blessings.

In the end, I can only believe that Ronnie must have awakened to a deeper spirit that had always been within him. It was this that must have given him the vision and courage to just say no to the war propaganda that had manipulated so many of us for too long.

Historians might say that he only initiated *glasnost* because it was good politics at the time. Or that it was economic: we were going broke in the Cold War. Our businessmen needed peaceful access to the markets in Eastern Europe. We were tired of the whole thing.

Whatever, it took a broad-gauge man to swallow his own words about "evil", make a 180 degree turn away from everything he'd been led to believe, and come down finally on the side of humanity.

The old Evil Empire was gone, but what lay ahead? More demons?

As some wag cracked when the grotesque little Telletubby dolls were introduced: "Be very afraid."

Sonoita, AZ, Thanksging Day, 2001: A friend and his wife are coming back from fishing down in Mexico. When they hit this busy border crossing into the U.S., they expect to find a long line of cars and heavy security, due to September 11th. To their surprise, they get through fairly quickly. A Customs Officer leans into the open window of their SUV and asks pleasantly: "Are you folks bringing in any aliens?" No. "Do you have any firearms?" No. "Do you have any weapons of mass destruction?"

"Yes," says my friend, "my wife." Then he's scared. To joke about something as grave as terrorism? Will they strip his vehicle and maybe jug him?

"Giddouta here." The officer grins and thumbs him on through to home.

EXPOSING WAR PROPAGANDA: 2

"Suppose They Gave a War and Nobody Came?"

I first heard that line chanted by long-haired radical kids protesting Vietnam. Now certainly I'd been an opponent of the war in Vietnam, but I was anything but ready for the outrage that roared up from our streets and campuses in the Sixties Revolution. It maddened me, these pot-headed dirty draft dodgers savaging our national policy. Burning our flag, tearing apart everything we hold dear in America. Gutless bastards, love it or leave it. Above all, don't you dare joke about it. This is sacred.

Vietnam is our survival.

The protesters had struck on a homespun antidote to the propaganda of war. Humor is an irresistible weapon to puncture the party line lie. The foreign policy elites are super-smart people. For all the facts and figures an ordinary citizen throws at them, they'll argue him or her down every time. But to laugh at them, make fun of their twists and turns—that they can't take. Dirty pool. Humor is truth. It makes the bewildered herd think.

155

Protest songs like A Draft Dodgers Rag, or <u>Where Have</u> <u>All the Flower Gone</u> probably influenced more minds than a hundred cruise missiles.

To resist war propanda is a conscious action. Take a current example, President Bush saying: "This is a 50-year war against evil."

When that statement strikes your consciousness—which operates like a computer—you scroll to Find in your data base. Your consciousness is binary like a computer. It can only give you a "yes" or "no" answer. Something is either true or it's false. No maybes. Your computer asks: is the statement true? If you enter True, instantly your computer pulls up its Memory Hole File which says to you: "Hey, look! Evil is back with us again. Didn't they try that same line with the commies? And the 50 years? The Cold War was only 44, so this baby is going to be worse. Cold War image? Right on! They're selling you a new endless war. True or False? Answer please. Hell no, you cry, I'm not suckering into that scam again! You punch in False and delete the lie.

What's comic-tragic about it—is the public really expected to believe that the U.S. is going to conquer Evil in 50 years? Brave new world. Christ has had 2001 years, and we still had September 11th. Then add Vice-President Cheney repeating in three separate speeches that more American citizens were going to die in this war than our troops overseas. "Bush and his buddies," writes the alternative magazine <u>In These Times</u>, "want us all in such a state of fear that we would gladly give up the cherished freedoms our forefathers fought for if it would prevent another September 11th."

What the citizen comes to realize is that there is a sub-text to the majority of our foreign policy actions. Why, for example, did the first President Bush attack Panama? Was it really to "get" Noriega, as the U.S. is now going to "get" binLaden? On TV, the public was not shown the rubbling of Panama by smart bombs or the considerable civilian casualties. It was rarely mentioned that Noreiga had been a CIA drug-running "asset" for years. Instead, the public was shown the vile man's secret lair, a ravaged office that had "cocaine" in it, a spooky voodoo altar and a scatter of obscene pictures of naked women in depraved copulation.

If citizens had had their memory hole open, if they'd taught themselves how to resist war propaganda—they would have recalled that the entire Noriega office scene was a re-run. Noriega's office, even down to the same desk and dirty pictures, had been used by the CIA as the reason to destroy democratically elected President Allende in Chile.

The sub-text for blasting Panama was simply more Grand Area-New World Order U.S. terrorism. Noriega was the scapegoat demon, the straw man. Under treaty a century ago, the U.S. had agreed to hand the Panama Canal back to Panama in the year 2000, provided that the Panamanian government would build its own defense force to protect it. So Noriega built exactly such a force, which the U.S. then went in and destroyed. Now Washington could say, Panama broke its treaty with us, so we have to garrison the place with U.S. troops. They're still there and always will be. As for drug-running out of Panama—Noriega's "sin"—the Panamanian puppet government the U.S. installed is, according to a UN report, currently shipping twice the amount of drugs out of Panama than Noreiga ever dreamed of. He's cooling his heels in an American prison, trying to figure out what hit him.

There was also a subtext when we attacked the demon "Slobo" (a Slob?) in Yugoslavia. The day we began bombing Kosovo, the NY <u>Times</u> reported: "One argument President Clinton used to justify the air war was that we needed a prosperous Europe that was 'a good partner with us for trading.'"

Trading partners are business, transnational corporations. A day or so later, Clinton's scriptwriters deleted the embarrassing trading partner blooper and replaced it with the more marketable "humanitarian" theme that would play in River City. Idealism. We'd be preventing genocide.

Pinedale, Wyoming, August 1991: About twenty of us are gathered for lunch in a cowboy restaurant in Wyoming. One of our senators has come out to talk to us about the meaning of Saddam's sudden invasion of Kuwait. Great fellow, this senator, one of the leaders in Congress, bright, funny, We often talk old times. Our grandfathers had been coal-mining neighbors in Wyoming. Honest, western, he stands up and says: "Now folks, we're not going to let Saddam get away with this. We're going to take him out in very short order. We'll absolutely flatten him in three or four days. But first I'm going to tell you what this war is about. It's not about money. It's not about oil. It's about getting rid of a new Hitler."

The woman sitting beside me sighs. She's a German, married to an American. During the war, her father and eleven of her uncles had been German generals. They were all killed. "When I was young," she whispers to me, "I was a rabid Hitler youth. We were so terribly propagandized to die for the Fuhrer that if I'd ever caught my parents listening to British radio or the American station, I would have turned them in to the Gestapo." She clutches my arm. "But what you don't realize is how propagandized you Americans are! That man—" she points at the lanky, affable senator—"is setting you up for war!"

We went. Less than a week later, Desert Storm.

According to John Stockwell, the former decorated CIA officer: "In the Persian Gulf, the White House has engineered a *causus belli*, a reason for justifying war against Iraq. Through Kuwait, the CIA had been destabilizing Iraq. During the Iran/Iraq war of the 1980's, Kuwait advanced its border further north and seized valuable Iraqi oil reserves. By manipulating oil prices, Kuwait cost Iraq billions of dollars in revenues. Meanwhile, on the eve of Iraq's invasion of Kuwait, the U.S. ambassador gave Saddam Hussein what seemed to be tacit reassurance that the United States would not respond. Had Hussein asked me," Stockwell, who worked with Bush in CIA, continues, "I would have assured him that President Bush would respond vigorously. He was shopping around for a war."

Foreign policy scholar Seymour Melman, professor emeritus at Columbia University and Chairman of the National Commission for Economic Conversion, asked at the time: "Why is Bush rushing down the path to another wasteful, destructive war? Oil supply is no issue.

The Administration is crying wolf about oil. The real objective in the Persian Gulf is to achieve a permanent military presence to dominate the area. This would justify a continuation of enormous military budgets that ensure the prosperity of military industry, as well as the power of Bush, now the CEO of the military-industrial complex. Such policies have gutted the U.S. economy. The war economy from 1949-1989 used up $8.2 trillion of resources of every kind—this exceeded the value of all U.S. industry and infrastructure which was $7.3 trillion."

Just as in the Vietnam tragedy, when I'd tried to expose the deception being sold to the public, in the Gulf War I wrote newspaper articles questioning U.S. motives. Earlier, I'd done some writing for the <u>Los Angeles Times</u> syndicate. In a short op-ed piece, I presented some of the facts that had been buried in our rush to war. A day or two later, an apologetic editor called me. "I loved what you wrote," he said. "I agree with it, but unfortunately we can't run it."

"Oh? How come?"

"We've had orders from up top: we can't print anything about the Gulf War unless the spokesman is a senior government or military official, which you are not."

Shortly thereafter, I talked to a former <u>Time</u> editor-in-chief. I congratulated him that the magazine had the guts to print an anti-war editorial by a woman writer who's a respected radical. He sniffed: "If I were still running the magazine, she wouldn't have been in there."

King City, California, 1991: a small restaurant, weekly meeting of the local Rotary. Now that the Gulf War is almost over, they've asked me to "give them the other side." Though they're a little suspicious of my oddball radical views, many of the Rotarians are friends of mine, fellow cattle ranchers or men I've hunted quail with. Good guys. One comes up to me and proudly plucks at the new jacket his wife has made for him. It's a silken rendition of Old Glory, glistening with stars and stripes. Yellow ribbons are on the tables. I've been scheduled to talk for a half hour on how the U.S. has been rushed into war, but just before I take the dais, there's an apologetic interruption. A senior girl from the high school has been invited in to recount the progress of the youth program the Rotary has been working on. Poor little thing is shy, fumbling out columns of numbers. When she finishes, I have five minutes left to show why we're burying our heads in the desert sand.

Shortly after September 11th, the American Cardinals met and endorsed the U.S. attack on terrorism. One Cardinal stated: "God is with us as we, with other allied nations, seek to defend the common good of our nations as well as the international common good and peace throughout the world."

"There is much that is troubling about the 'God is with us' banner in wartime," replied the <u>National Catholic Reporter.</u> "Warriors always claim God as they enter conflict. What kind of God would do anything but weep? Nations not only lose wisdom in war, they lose nuance as well. Dissenting voices become unpopular and marginalized, yet are needed more than ever.

"The reaction of Asian Christians to the American bombing was not enthusiastic. The heads of the Coptic church and the Egyptian Catholic church condemned the bombings as arrogant, wrong and against international law. Said church groups in New Delhi, 'the terrorist attacks should be a wake-up call, not a call to battle.'

"By dropping the bombs, a police action has been elevated into an all-out military assault—moral discrimination is out the window. Osama bin Laden is elevated from a hateful terrorist, a criminal mastermind, to a one-man superpower. As Anglican Bishop Peter Forster and other clerics worldwide warn: "The common good does not end at the borders of powerful Western nations."

In a report to the 105th Congress, the Cato Institute, a libertarian policy group in Washington, opposed the posting of U.S. troops in Saudi Arabia and America's military commitment to the Persian Gulf as a whole. "The United States currently buys $11 billion of Gulf oil per year, yet U.S. taxpayers spend $40 to $50 billion (some analysts estimate as much as $70 billion) per year to defend the region."

Adds Professor Gregory Gause III, a member of the Middle East Policy Council, "No matter who governs these countries, they have to sell us oil. They can't drink the stuff. It's the only thing they have." According to an econometric study conducted by David Henderson, an economic adviser to President Reagan, "If Saddam Hussein had taken control of not only Kuwait's oil supply, but had also invaded Saudi Arabia and the United Arab Emirates, the United States gross domestic product would have dropped only.5% because of higher oil prices."

Ivan Eland, director of defense policy studies at the Cato Institute, sums up the Gulf War: "We said we were fighting for oil but we basically shot ourselves in the foot." Later UN sanctions on Iraqi oil sales have taken much more oil off the world market than the Iraqi invasion of Kuwait ever threatened to. "We got a patriotic feeling from a great tactical victory, but did we actually win there? Saudi Arabia has a much larger military budget than Iraq's. Even if Iraq is a threat—and there's a lot of question whether Iraq could mount an attack—why can't these countries that have bigger GDP than Iraq defend themselves? We shouldn't be more concerned about their defense than they are. If the terrorist attack on us had never happened, the question would be: do we really need to spend money to defend oil in Saudi Arabia? Most economists would say no."

Nicholas Berry, a senior analyst with the Center for Defense Information puts it this way: "Every Islamic country, from Indonesia all the way to Morocco, is under some form of U.S. sanctions. We're often unilateral in our sanctions, which really allows the Japanese, the Italians, the French, whoever, to monopolize trade. And it builds resentment and that feeds terrorism. Our economic sanctions against Iraq have been particularly damaging, helping Saddam maintain his grip on power while harming the U.S. image in the Islamic world. The rationale is to keep Iraq poor so it cannot develop weapons of mass destruction that would threaten Israel."

In the confusion of motives surrounding the present war or any war—in the anger, pain and fear so many Americans feel—the public is baffled to know what course to take. Patriotism? God on our side? What flag to follow?

"In the current war," writes Colman McCarthy, formerly of the Washington <u>Post</u> and present director of the Center for Teaching Peace, "pacifists are asked, often goadingly: 'OK, you're opposed to violence, but what's your solution instead?' Fair question.

"We have a three part answer based on political, legal and moral solutions. Political: follow the U.S. government's long time advice to Israeli and Palestinian leaders: talk to each other, negotiate, deal, compromise, stop the killing and reconcile. Both China and Russia were demonized as regimes out to annihilate the U.S., threats far more lethal than the current demons, the ranting ragtag Taliban (which the U.S. armed and supported.) Now, because of negotiation, Russia and China are trading partners.

"Legal: Use international law and the World Court at the Hague where due process now has Slobodan Milosevic on trial. Moral response: Follow the core teachings of the historical figure President Bush claimed during his candidacy he most looked to for guidance. Jesus. Forgive the September 11th attackers for their violence, ask them to forgive the U.S. government for its long history of military and economic violence, and then seek reconciliation through mutual dialogue, not one-sided monologue."

Concluding on a personal note, McCarthy writes: "My own plan is to keep teaching and writing, and resisting the urge to blame those who believe violence is the solution to conflict, whether among nations, families or neighborhoods. I blame only one person for the persistence of violence: myself. If I work to be a better husband, father, teacher, writer and informed citizen, I've done all I can to try to decrease the world's violence and increase its peace."

"The roots of war," writes Thich Nhat Hanh, the Vietnamese Buddhist monk nominated for the Nobel Peace Prize, "are in the way we live our daily lives. The way we develop our industries, build our society, consume goods. We cannot just blame one side or the other. We need the vision of inter-being—we belong to each other. Every side is 'our side'—there is no evil side."

While the Cold War was still raging, Russian exile novelist Alexander Solzhenitsyn made a bold prediction:

"The triumph of inwardness (being), over outwardness (doing), will be a great turning point in the history of mankind, comparable to the transition from the Middle Ages to the Renaissance. There will be a complete change, not only in the direction of our interests and activities, but in the very nature of human beings, a change from spiritual dispersion to spiritual concentration. This ascension will be similar to climbing onto the next anthropological stage. No one on earth has any way left but upward."

Beyond the propaganda, beyond the furor of wars—a change of heart.

Cora, Wyoming, August 1990: We're sitting in the sun, looking down on the Green River that flows through our ranch. "You left out the important part," says the blonde woman beside me.

"Oh? What's that?"

"You know perfectly well." She pierces me with her frank, incisive blue eyes. "You've got to tell what changed you."

I groan inwardly. All lazy authors like me dread revisions, and she's talking about a life story. Yet I so admire her and respect her opinion, I've got to listen. Ruth Adams, for years, has been editor of the <u>Bulletin of Atomic Scientists</u>. She probably knows more about national security than most of the defense specialists who are her contributors. Her husband, Robert McCormick Adams, a former director of the Smithsonian also happens to be my older brother's brother in law. So, tugging on family ties and old friendship, I've prevailed on Ruth to give me her opinion of a political tome I've written: <u>Giving up War.</u>

"We have much the same background," she continues, "know the same people. But why is it you don't think like them? You don't have the same values. The reader wants to know what made you change."

"I've never thought much about it. Too much heavy lifting."

"Then you better start thinking, put it in. People are interested in that kind of stuff—particularly if they want to change themselves."

LIVING IN POSITIVE,
NOT NEGATIVE EMOTIONS

<u>Giving Up War</u> never comes out. For all the facts, figures and exhortations I'd put in, publisher after publisher rejected it. The book had been written in the midst of the Cold War which the editors assured me was going to go on for years, Any book claiming otherwise was just not realistic. But the main reason for rejecting the book, they added, was that mankind will never be able to give up war. It's too deeply imbedded in human nature.

Back to square one. I was saddened that I seemed to be so out of step with prevailing opinion. I wondered if I were acting like the cranky old Irishman, Pat, who'd just become a U.S. citizen. Somebody asks him: "Well, Pat, now that you can vote, what are you going to be? Republican?"

"Wouldn't be caught dead!"

"Democrat, then?"

"Not on your life, laddie!"

173

"But Pat, you've got to be something!"

"Aren't I, though! A'gin' the guv'mint I am!"

My problem was, I loved my government and my country. I dreaded being an oddball going against my peers. As LBJ is reputed to have said, "You don't want to be a camel pissing outside the tent. Piss on the inside and it means something."

So, as Ruth Adams asked, why the change? How did I get this way?

Maybe Governor Lamm of Colorado once put his finger on it when he said, "Peace is not the absence of war. Peace is a change of heart." And Tolstoy before him: "Everybody thinks about changing humanity. Nobody thinks about changing himself."

The fatal flaw in my Giving Up War, I've come to realize, was that while I was arguing *facts* in the book, my readers were reacting with *emotions*. Emotions are the cause of war. Only by rising out of the lower emotions into the higher ones could my change or perhaps anyone's take place. What changed me must have been when forces within me caused me slowly and painfully, finding and losing, to begin rising to a higher healing level of consciousness. This was an emotional step, a listening to an inner voice that some call common sense, and others, spirit, soul.

Once touched by it, the world indeed begins to look different.

Like every human being, Teddy and I were raised with the values of our parents and our particular culture. Though she was Southern from Memphis and I was a damn Yankee from Chicago, our upbringings were quite similar. We came from reasonably affluent families, went to the "good" and "right" schools. We were bred to be ladies and gentlemen and someday, if possible, leaders in our society. Raise our children according to the same tribal code, get out in the world, run a corporation or law office, earn money, amount to something. Vote conservative Republican, love our country and love God. Amen.

That mindset lasted until our early married years. In a real tearing—leaving family, friends and the security of our life—we moved away from our home turf and struck out on our own. Strange choice of words. Three strikes and you're out. Sometimes we surely were out, of sight and of mind. As a writer, I was pretty much on the fringe anyway—"no money in it," my father used to remind me. He begged me to get into "legitimate business." Do the acceptable thing. The "respectable" thing, which was more or less the driving force for the descendents of once poor Irish immigrants. "Three generations, shirt-sleeves to shirt-sleeves," my mother used to warn. Or, when she'd finally accepted my "writing" after I'd had a novel chosen by a major book club, she acquiesced with the old Irish phrase, "Well, I suppose it's a poor family that can't afford one gentleman."

But Teddy has always done her own thing. As a descendant of the John Smith family of Pocahontas fame in the Virginia Colony, she had no status or performance ethic to serve. She was always a free spirit regarding what people thought about her. What you see is what you get. When she became a convert to Catholicism so that we could be married in "my church," her Episcopal family groaned and her old black nurse said, "Miss Frederika, that Mister Otis is not only a damn Yankee but an Irish Catholic damn Yankee."

From childhood on, Teddy had always had a strong spiritual yearning. It wasn't particularly churchy, it was sometimes emotional but always caring: it was just who she was. A friend once told her: "You've found your way. It's devotion." As for me, a cradle Catholic, I not only squirmed through ritual but was pretty much a come-day-go-day-God-rush-payday believer. When Teddy began really digging into the works of the spiritual masters, she exposed me, often kicking and fighting, to concepts of the spirit that I hadn't wanted to think about or even knew existed.

Thomas Merton was one of her favorites. "The wars, cataclysms and plagues," he wrote, "that convulse human society are in reality the outward expression of a hidden spiritual battle. To be consciously and spiritually committed to the worldly power struggle in business, politics and war is to founder in darkness, confusion and sin."

Such words focused us on the meaning of life, and thus questioned the materialistic preoccupations of so much in our society. This was hard going. Slowly we found ourselves at odds with many of the values of men and women whom we admired and were our best friends. We loved them all and still do. It was just that they seemed to have their eyes on a different goal. Far from being some "born again" conversion, with the smugness of "we know, and you don't," we just felt that we'd been born with something that was no credit to us and at times actually painful because it separated us from so much we'd held dear.

Once we'd moved out onto cattle ranches, Teddy began teaching catechism in a rural parochial school. Then she helped organize a food bank for migrant Hispanic field workers. The quiet of the land, the remoteness and healing cycles of nature all played a part in expanding our view of the meaning of life. What were we really put here for? As Emerson said, "You can have truth or repose. You cannot have both." By then, at an occasional party with old friends, we not only didn't agree with their politics and values, but we felt we were almost spies, "passing" in a world that was not ours anymore.

During the Cold War, I read Jonathan Schell's <u>Fate of the Earth.</u> The enormity of the nuclear challenge and the problem of violence really hit home. Almost from that moment, I decided that what little I could do in writing would at least now be directed toward trying to shed light on some of these major issues. I became increasingly anti-war and read everything I could dig out. Howard Zinn's classic <u>Peoples History of the United States</u>, Noam Chomsky's many works, Gore Vidal's, Jonathan Kwitny's <u>Endless Enemies</u>, William Greider's <u>Who Will Tell the People</u>? From these and many more, I began to sense a common need for citizen activism and change. Everything I wrote was influenced by a gradual awakening to a larger view of behavior, conduct and governance.

It was sometime in there that I stumbled into the mysterious enigma of consciousness, both individual and collective.

Hollister, California, February, 1997: Small luncheon of a local women's club. They've asked me to talk about my new novel, <u>Frontiers</u>. It's the story of an Irish immigrant who from 1876 to 1945 fights in all the

American wars. Loves soldiers and hates war. But we never get to the book itself. It's more of a show and tell. The ladies want to see one of these strange writer ducks and find out what his life is like. To loosen them up, I begin by telling them some hopefully funny anecdotes, movie and TV experiences mostly. They listen politely enough, but nobody breaks up laughing. Tough audience so far. Then it occurs to me to mention my current struggle with one of my ego demons—the old fear of failure that had been activated by a collapsed deal with a network to make a series out of <u>Frontiers</u>. I had come across a line that had really helped me out of my doldrums:

"Happiness is less a matter of getting what you want than wanting what you have."

It's as if I've flung a hand-grenade into the room. Here now I'm talking about them, not merely spooling out my own funnies. These women aren't fancy or sophisticated. They're wives of ranchers, farmers, secretaries, local business owners. Grass-roots folks, innately shy, yet now their eyes whip to me. A few clap, others cry out, "Yes! That's true!"

I'm stunned. Why in hell could the simple words "wanting what you have" evoke such an emotional response? It was almost as if I've told them something they knew but didn't know they knew. When the speech is over, groups of them gather around me to talk about wanting what you have. One woman says, "When is enough enough?"

Instinctively, these women seemed to be seeking the truth about their meaning. Did they have to live restlessly wanting something from Out There? Or did they realize that they already had everything they needed, In Here, within themselves, and that was their power and their peace?

Havingness versus Wantingness. Power versus Force.

That day, I had a headstart on the women. I had been reading material from a remarkable pioneer in consciousness: David Hawkins, M.D. PhD. For nearly a year, I'd been working on a new book inspired by David,

The Victory of Surrender. The source of it was his own work, **Power versus Force: The Hidden Determinants of Human Behavior.**

David is no off-the-wall guru. At one time in New York, he had such a large psychiatric practice, with 35 psychiatric assistants and worldwide patients that Columbia-Presbyterian hospital had to build a new wing to accommodate them. He co-authored <u>Orthomolecular Psychiatry</u> with his friend, Nobel scientist Linus Pauling. Then, abandoning his lucrative practice and 80 acre Long Island estate, he moved to Arizona—Rattlebone Ranch, he calls his adobe hideaway. Here, he drives forty miles to treat abused Navajo girls, and devotes the rest of his time to writing seminal works on human consciousness.

His "Hidden Determinants of Human Behavior" are emotions. Centuries ago, the Perennial Philosophy of ancient sages and mystics had reflected on the power that emotions have on the way humans act.

The low-end emotions which he calls "the bottom of the box" determine your behavior. When you allow yourself to be controlled by the negative emotions of guilt, apathy, grief, fear, desire, anger and pride, your body knows that you're living in wantingness. You're perpetually unfulfilled. You're wanting something Out There. You have to use force to get it. Your electrical energy goes negative, at times even suppressing your immune system.

However, when you live in the "top of the box" high-end positive emotions, courage, neutrality, willingness, acceptance, reason, love, joy and peace, your body knows that you're living in havingness. You're fulfilled. In this moment now you already have everything you need. You take back your power. It's In Here, with you. You create your own happiness. Your electrical energy goes positive. Your immune systems respond.

Our behaviors are mirrored in the structures we make. If we live in fear, we build fortresses of fear in which to hunker down and defend ourselves. If, as he estimates, 85% of humanity still lives in negative low-end emotions, think what effect that has on our politics, business, war and society in general. The Drug War, for instance, is motivated primarily by the negative emotions of Shame,

Fear and Anger. To heal effectively, it would have to rise to the level of Acceptance.

Hawkins believes that 85% of our physical ills (and to me, our national ones) are caused by our living in the low end emotions. He says:

"Subtle grades of depression kill more people than all other diseases of mankind combined. There is no anti-depressant that will cure a depression that is spiritually based, because the malaise does not originate from brain dysfunction but from an accurate response to the desecration of life. The body is a reflection of the spirit in its physical expression, and its problems are the dramatization of the struggles of the spirit which gives it life."

I thought again of the reactions of the women to my speech. Were their emotions triggered by the phrase "wanting what you have?" Was that the truth that they responded to, and was the lie the "getting what you want" that most of us, present company definitely included, have spent most of our lives trying to do?

What American doesn't believe in getting? Happiness has to be getting what we want. To do so, we've been trained to compete, to control. These ordinary small-town women were no more avaricious than anyone else, in fact, probably less so because they lived outside the mainstream. Yet few of us can escape the influence of our culture. In myriad ways, desire has been hot-wired into us. Wantingness. Wanting something out there that somebody must give us, and if not, we have to use force to get it. Our schools, government, media and families relentlessly teach us that our purpose in life is to win. We're in a war. Victory is beating the system so that it showers on us our fair share of money, power, fame or possessions. These are clearly the rewards our society reveres. If you get them, you're a winner. You're somebody. You're worth something.

If you fail to get them, you're a loser. Nobody. Occupant. No worth as a human being.

But my few random words must have struck down this cultural lie. Instinctively, the womens' bodies *knew* that our belief system of getting has brought us only flashes of happiness against a darkening sky of increasing disillusionment.

Millions of us suffer from actual or imagined physical ills. We're the most medicated people on earth, yet few of us heal.

An estimated three-quarters of us mistrust our government. For many of us, our system doesn't seem to be working. Our traditional values are eroding. We don't quite know where we are or how we got there. More and more we feel depersonalized. We respond to the desecration of our lives in fear, doubt and rage, yet we don't know what to do about it.

As a people accustomed to getting our way—winning—it now appears that we've tried to force our will on ourselves, our nation and the world. When we fail, when nothing changes, we're bound to feel powerless. By trying to control events out there, over which we have no control, we have lost our power in here, in ourselves. We're programming our consciousness computer with software of the past or the future. We're grieving about what we didn't get yesterday, or we're fearing what we might not get tomorrow.

We're making our happiness conditional on people or events that had been or will be. Thus, we've cut ourselves off from the only true happiness any human can ever know: to live in this moment right now.

Our cultural lifestyle of wantingness is a dead end. We never get "there" because, as Gertrude Stein said, "there is no there there." "There" is forever dependent on someone else or some event giving us something in the future. We never get enough of what we want, whether it's money, power, fame or things. Thus, we rob ourselves of the precious moment of the present, the exact now where we can discern truth and what we really are.

The result?

Lives of quiet desperation. Distracted from distraction by distractions. Play catch up ball. Smile the smile of friendly unhappiness. Have a nice day. Make my day. Get a life. When we can't control the "out there," can't get our way, we as individuals and nation respond in frustration, fear and sickening.

Our bodies have been reacting by reflex to the lie we are living. Our emotions are responsible for imprisoning us in the darkness of wantingness. The media, particularly TV advertising, has swamped us with hundreds of sales messages around the clock, and if we buy, our rising expectations are usually unfulfilled. But the leap to Courage requires us to face the truth about ourselves, own up to our weakness, neediness and inflated self-images that are all the common clay of human behavior. Admit them, forgive them and go on. Should enough of us re-program ourselves to live in the higher emotions of havingness, isn't it possible that by healing ourselves, we might also begin to heal our nation?

The emotions of Desire and Pride, for example, are played upon by advertisers to induce us to buy their products. We make ourselves vulnerable to the materialism of our culture when we allow ourselves to be controlled by these negative emotions which inflame our Wantingness.

More important in a national sense, war propaganda from our government is designed to appeal to the low end emotions of Shame, Grief, Anger and Pride. There is Wantingness here, too. We want desperately to be protected. We allow ourselves to sink into Shame when the violence of a September 11th attacks us. Are we so soft or cowardly that we can't even defend ourselves? Then we act out Grief for all the anguish we've suffered. And once mourned, we hurl ourselves into raging Anger. Do something! Hit back! Our Pride has been insulted. Plant our flag on the ramparts and show the world how brave Americans are!

Now, patriotism is a noble force, the most powerful bonding mechanism in human experience. Millions of brave men and women have died for it.

But there's also a grave risk in it, a downside that has become painfully evident in the U.S. response to September 11th.

"I'm a warmonger," writes Greg Dobbs, an award-winning correspondent for ABC News, "but peace is not a dirty word. Nor is protest. Yet right now in America those who protest for peace are called disloyal, their patriotism questioned. Take the American Council of Trustees and Alumni, founded by Lynne Cheney, wife of the vice-president and an accomplished leader in her own right.

"It has compiled a McCarthyesque list of American university professors it considers anti-American. Why?

Because they have raised questions about the war on terrorism, concerns about American foreign policy. They have not toed the company line.

"Well, I fly my flag to commemorate a country in which you can articulate your alarm without endorsing the enemy. A country in which you don't have to toe the company line to be a patriot. In which dissent is a proud tradition, not shameful treachery. Where you qualify as a real American simply by caring about your country, right or wrong. And saying so—because you can."

Lynne Cheney is a thoughtful, active woman who has worked hard to serve the common good. But she is reacting to our grave security situation now out of fear.

There are hopeful signs that a broader, all-inclusive kind of caring, an emotional change of heart is already happening. Denis Kucinich, congressman from Ohio, in a speech at the University of California addressed the fear and panic that we have seen since September 11:

"I offer these brief remarks today as a prayer for our country, with love of democracy, as a celebration of our country. With love for our country. With hope for our country. With a belief that the light of freedom cannot be extinguished as long as it is inside of us. With a belief that freedom rings resoundingly in a democracy each time we speak freely. With the understanding that freedom stirs the human heart and fear stills it. With the belief that a free people cannot walk in fear and faith at the same time. With the understanding that there is a deeper truth expressed in the unity of the United States. That implicit in the union of our country is the union of all people. That all people are essentially one. That the world is interconnected not only on the material level of economics, trade, communication, and transportation, but *innerconnected* through human consciousness, through the human heart, through the heart of the world, through the simply expressed impulse and yearning to be and to breathe free. I offer this prayer for America."

The mystic, Ingo Swann, who predicted the end of the Berlin Wall 18 months before it happened, is world-renowned for his ability to tap into consciousness. He writes: "The completeness of the failure of most 20th century systems, mindsets and affiliated institutions will result in a great sense of betrayal and great, unifying anger. It is out of this great anger that the centralizing, re-empowering highest values of the third millenium will arise. These values will not remotely resemble those of the 20th century."

The history of the United States shows that a change of national heart is not only possible but that our nation was founded on it.

In 1776, what people called America was a captive nation, enslaved by Great Britain in a system of economic and military domination. But despite how unjust and brutal the system was, the vast majority of colonists were afraid to give it up. It was the devil they knew. But then, like now, change was in the air. Only eleven percent of the colonists were open to these winds of change, yet the rising spirit of that eleven percent made the American Revolution happen.

The Declaration of Independence calibrates in the highest emotional levels of enlightenment. The words of Lincoln's Gettysburg Address have exactly the same liberating effect on our psyches. We were indeed in Lincoln's time "the last best hope on earth."

What about today, now?

Psychologists estimate that it only takes about 25% of a population "getting it" before they demand changes in their system. Surprisingly, even despite our present problems, recent polls show that an estimated one-quarter of Americans have already risen high enough in consciousness, into the healing emotions, that they're seeking a society of spiritual enlightenment and a total break with the old mindsets and methods of governance. Such men and women are beginning to live their search for truth, whether it's in addicts anonymous groups in every town in the land, or in thinking locally in community betterment, or thinking globally in protecting the environment that belongs to us all, these people are "walking their talk," as the New Agers say.

Their human spirit is telling them just say no to the bondage of the past, the atrocities of violence, the induced fears and the wantingness of desires.

The ancient enslavements of mankind—divine right of kings, degredation of women, slavery and imperialism—were founded in negative emotions, and thus creating systems that had been accepted as a natural part of life. They were ended when a small percentage of humans rose high enough into enlightenment to choose between truth or lie. These were major leaps in consciousness just as the Declaration of Independence was such a leap.

"Salvation lies in the effort," said Gandhi, "not the attainment. Full effort is full victory."

Empowered, he and millions like him took peaceful action as citizens and ended the British Empire's enslavement of India.

It can happen here—I believe it will happen—when enough of us come together in a new commitment to the actions needed to change our beloved nation's heart.

Cora, Wyoming, October 1, 2001: I'm walking beside the frozen yellow willows on the bank of the Green. The river is black, motionless, hardly a ripple, the water so low I'm not even shooting ducks this year. There are too few in the drought.

Yet there is still water, still life in this historic river. Say goodbye to it now until spring—Teddy and I about to head south to the other ranch our son operates in Arizona. And say thanks, too, count our blessings.

Thirty-three years ago, politics tried to take the river away from us. Build a giant dam just downstream. Turn our ranch and those of our neighbors into a giant mudflat reservoir. But we fought back, all of us together, wrote a brochure about the vital habitat that would be lost here. We had no power, just ordinary local citizens, hunters, fishermen, schoolteachers, old grizzled ranchers who believed the government was all crooked anyway so why fight it? But fight we do. Take our case to Cheyenne, fail there, then to Washington. Hang in for months and finally doom the dam.

Below me, three bull moose, pursuing a cow moose with a calf, plunge into the icy water. The sun glints on the back of a big brown trout. He slaps his tail, says goodbye and heads south, too. But the river lives on. Somebody cared.

TAKING POLITICAL ACTION

It's a long way from a local victory to a national one, but the principle is the same.

It's the caring—that's what the citizen can do to end the violence.

One by one, ordinary Americans awakening to band together, committing themselves to help activate the dismantling of failed systems of the past and replacing them with a truly democratic governance that equally, with fairness and patience, comes to represent the interests of all Americans.

September 11th was a tragic wake-up call to every citizen that the time is now to take the political responsibility that is the national birthright of each of us. To stand up and be counted. Renew the American Dream in its original vision, a society of justice, peace and hope, a better tomorrow for the life, liberty and pursuit of happiness of every citizen.

To make this happen, it's not enough to just say no, to sit on the sidelines and carp about a better world. To attain it, the citizen activist movement has to say yes—to humility, openness, compassion and vision. And to work toward correcting the inequities of the past where, too often, the interests of the few have controlled the lives of the many.

Washington, August, 2001: a citizen has become concerned about a war-related federal program that he feels must be stopped in the national interest. He writes his senator several times. When he gets only a form-letter explanation, he goes at his own expense to Washington and confronts the senator in his office. "Why is it," he asks him, "you're still pushing for this ridiculous, harmful program?"

The senator reaches into his desk and pulls out a file. "I have to listen," he said. "There's a landslide in favor of the program."

"Landslide?" the citizen asks. "What's a landslide?"

The senator upends the file and dumps out eight letters.

Exercising responsibility as an American citizen means getting involved. Caring what's going on in the country.

T.S. Eliot wrote a maxim for life: "Teach us to care, and not to care." In other words, care with all one's heart, work hard, get in and give it one's best shot. And then—like David Hawkins next higher level in consciousness: Detachment—"not care." The citizen has done everything he or she can. "The rest," as Eliot puts it, "is not our business."

There's a tremendous healing power in such detachment. I've found in my own life that not caring frees me from making demons out of people and systems I can't control or beat. When your detachment has made you give up your "I know," when it makes you rip off your fundamentalist blinders that try to tell you you've got to be Number One, be in Control, be Right—once you've lifted up to that level, you've added to your personal power. Strangely, your opponents recognize it as a quality they wish they had. The result: even if you fail in your particular project of caring, just your effort has added to the enlightenment of your opponent. The energy of your effort has gone out into the database of collective consciousness. When enough citizens are making that effort, their sheer act of caring could well be influencing the universe in ways none of us will ever know.

Citizen action is cumulative. It's like you're one tiny ripple, but when you plop down your effort on the sand, it sucks in a slightly larger ripple behind you, then more and more ripples join and become waves, until soon they've swollen up into coamers, and when the sea is angry enough, it roars up into a tsunami. That's the process of what the citizen can do, and if and when the tidal wave happens, the hope is that it will clean a lot of dead wood off of our golden shores.

Howard Zinn's <u>Peoples History of the United States</u>—recommended reading for the citizen activist— shows in its fascinating pages how protest movements in our country have historically become so powerful that they've had to be incorporated into our national culture. That's the true strength and the genius of our American system. Whether it's for the rights of labor, women,

African Americans, if their wheels squeak loudly enough, the nation finally broadens its system and includes them.

There is no blueprint and shouldn't be for each citizen taking political action. Our true power is that we're all different, unique individuals with unique talents. One can write a book, another can write a protest song, others shoot home videos and grass roots documentaries.

Many protest sites are now springing up on the Web, millions of concerned activists communicating with each other, setting up websites like Empowermentproject.org. Some of them make films that appear on activist dish stations such as Free Speech TV, or World Link TV. This is not major TV network news, it's people news, the general public using information channels unknown a few years ago.

Some of the protest essays on the Internet are powerful and point toward thoughtful, realistic solutions. Talk radio, too, is an excellent loudspeaker for protest. Citizens are getting a message out there, each in his own way and abilities. One individual might say, I can't write good letters. I've never written my representatives. The wife and I don't have time to go to political meetings. But even if that citizen is not cut out for waving placards on the barricades, he or she still has a voice. They can still speak truth to power. Talk to their neighbors and friends, help them educate, activate themselves. Show them how, by rising in consciousness, they can take back their power and not let the system benumb them any longer in anomie and self-perceived apathy. The same goes for the citizen standing up and being counted in his or her company, union or church.

When the citizen has the courage to buck the system, just say no, there's often a reluctance, even a fear that one is leaving the tribe. It's a protective instinct in mankind that goes back to the caves. It's from the tribe that we derive our sense of worth, our understanding of what the community accepts and what it rejects. The tribe gives us our values, our truth. The bonding in the tribe is what makes civilization. Nobody wants to stand out there alone and say "I disagree" and suffer the enmity of those still inside the cave.

There are ways to tell the truth without being offensive. They should be part of a citizen activist's code.

Telling the truth should never become a control device: "I'm telling you what is right." This pitfall is probably the most destructive behavior in all organizations. The citizen can't be strident nor fundamentalist, hitting people over the head with his or her convictions. To keep control of anger-pride emotions requires practice and saintly patience. Noam Chomsky, the master political activist, never lets himself get personally involved in what he's saying. He simply says the truth like it is, and documents it. As we used to write for Jack Webb in Dragnet, "Just the facts, ma'am.

The other pitfall of citizen activism is that it can be boring. How much more fun to go out, shoot a round of golf or pop a top and watch the SuperBowl instead of sitting in eye-glazing meetings, talking back to bureaucrats, often for little or no reward. On the other hand, if a citizen won't do it, it means one less out there on the firing line. A political vacuum is created, and will be filled by those with the time, patience and money.

Then, too, many activist groups implode by trying to control the entire situation. This creates unrealistic expectations, excessive efforts and compulsive schedules. When goals become ego-driven, the center cannot hold. Dissension arises, egos do battle and the real mission is derailed by petty manipulations.

The citizen activist has to overcome his or her doubts about thinking differently than their peers and daring to say so. But again, it's Care and Not Care. You've told as much of the truth as you know. Nobody has the whole truth. All your spirit asks of you is to do your best, care your best. You aren't expected to re-make the world all by yourself. It will happen when it happens.

The upside is, being an involved citizen is personally exhilarating. Many people today, particularly the elderly, don't feel they have any value anymore to society, don't have anything left to do or any meaning in their lives. Hence, too often, they die simply out of boredom. Even the ones blessed with affluence soon tire of their shiny toys and their boredom can become overwhelming. How many rounds of golf can anyone play? How many Carnival cruises left to take, how many adult education courses? Isn't it deep down just killing time, waiting for the undertaker?

But if time is the doomsday clock, running on the country, as a patriot, the activist citizen has a mission. Generations of brave men and women have given their lives to preserve this blessed nation. The activist citizen has chosen to become part of that heroic stream.

Take the simple matter of writing elected representatives. Most people don't. Politics, they believe, is only influenced by numbers and power. While that is certainly true, the citizen activist is still one vote, still counts, particularly when he or she make that point crystal clear to their representatives. This can mean writing them, calling, and sometimes confronting them in person. Being the squeaky wheel they may dislike but can't ignore. When they're stumping for re-election, citizen activists are going to be there in the room, holding their representatives feet to the fire with questions they have to answer thoughtfully or risk losing a vote. Enough probing questions and the message gets through.

The average citizen feels powerless because the overwhelming money of corporations and financial elites has taken his destiny out of his hands and has convinced him that his vote is meaningless. The cost of a political seat is so huge that no one can get to Washington without being in someone's pocket.

It's amusing to hear politicians promising to cut Big Government. How can they when it's they themselves? A politician pretending to attack the corporate state is cutting off his money nose to spite his face.

Charles Derber, a professor of sociology and political analyst writes in his <u>Corporation Nation:</u> "Corporations help create our growing obsession with money and success, molding both our morality and material lives. Moving beyond a corporate-dominated world will require toppling the gods of consumerism and hypermaterialism, and building a new culture in which human values take priority over market priorities. Our new politics must change the codes and practices of corporations and governments as well as individuals— while at the same time protecting the health of business enterprise itself."

It's a matter of balance. We need industry, production, products. We need livelihoods that corporations provide. Our creative business initiatives and corporate efficiency not only have given Americans the highest standard of living in the world, but have enhanced the lives of the millions who have come here. But we also need lives that are not desecrated and dehumanized by the increasing, often ruthless corporate values that focus mainly on the bottom line.

To correct this inequity, many proposals are on the table. Remove all donor money from the political process, no PACS, no gifts, no "clients" whose money clout shapes policies for their own ends, not for the common good. Limited federal funds alone would finance congressional and presidential elections.

The political power of corporations will have to be limited. In the early days of our nation, corporations were chartered by the state to perform a specific mission. If it didn't enhance the common good, the state had the power to revoke the corporate charter. Recently, however, some of the finest legal minds in the nation have won court decisions stating that a corporation has exactly the same rights as an individual.

"The publicly traded, limited liability corporation," says corporate analyst David Korten, "is an institutional form programmed by its legal structure to behave like a sociopath irrespective of the ethical sensibilities of the employees who serve it, including those of the CEO." Corporations claim they have the citizen's right of free speech, but what is free or fair about a corporation dumping millions into political campaigns when an average citizen has trouble scraping up ten dollars to pay his party dues. Though there are certainly different emphases in the platforms of the Republican and Democratic parties—how each would solve problems— still, the entire political game is the bottom line, and basically a rich man's club. The average citizen is not only out of it but he's not expected to play.

During the last election campaign, a corporate CEO gave a luncheon for a small group of his friends. He expected that they might pledge a half million dollars for their presidential candidate. Imagine his surprise when this handful of executives put up a million two hundred thousand. They didn't feel it. The average compensation of American CEO's is $13 million a year, much of it in stock options. If he makes money for his company, its stock price increases. E.g.: if his eye is on the bottom line, he puts more in his own pocket. In 1990 in Japan, the average CEO was paid about 11 times more than his lowest employee. Here, his American counterpart is paid 211 times more, and often in excess of that.

No one denies that our corporations have made tremendous contributions to our welfare at home and to enhancing lives all over the world. Yet it's also true that no individual can stand up against the massive power and wealth of a corporation. It is an artificial, wholly undemocratic construct that can pretty much do as it pleases anywhere in the world. And if blocked by political resistance at home, it can threaten politicians that it will move its entire structure overseas, not only avoiding U.S. taxes but disemploying tens of thousands of workers.

According to Ralph Nader, "The Department of Commerce concedes that at least 360,000 jobs have been lost under NAFTA, and private research groups estimate the total may be twice that number." A sense of responsibility to the common good is not on the corporate agenda. Hopefully, changes to limit corporate power will be embraced by far-sighted corporations themselves before outraged citizen action forces them to do so.

A small, close to home example: recently, the Ford corporation through the Ford Foundation gave $5 million to a national conservation organization whose announced mission was to remove all livestock grazing on public lands in the Southwest. When a group of ranchers, livestock organizations and small-town Ford dealers finally sat down with a Ford representative, they said in effect: on one hand you advertise in our publications telling us we ought to buy Fords, then on the other hand you back an organization that's trying to put us out of business. Do you have any idea of all the rural towns you'll turn ghost, of the unemployment you'll cause, of the generations-old livelihoods you'll destroy? Why would you do such a thing?

In embarrassment, the Ford representatives said, They didn't know why the grant had been made, except that it was kind of a fuzzy, "feel good" thing. Astounded by citizen pressure, Ford backed away from the gift.

In national politics, to effect a truly representative government of citizen legislators, it has been suggested that perhaps one third of the Congress be chosen out of the general public and elected for short terms on a grand jury type system. If grand juries of ordinary people, our peers, can decide our life or death, why not the destiny of our nation? This would break the cycle of a political elite being constantly kept in office, virtually captives of vested interests who support them. A corollary is that the President would be elected for one six year term only, that he wouldn't spend much of his term making the pay-back deals necessary for re-election. He's in for six years and at the end he goes home, permanently.

What the average citizen often fails to realize is that economic/political power is a web that ensnares us all—and most particularly, the 80% of the bewildered herd who are seen not to count. Money in politics, corporate influence on the electoral process, aggrandizement of the military-industrial complex, massive media power and a lop-sided tax policy are all strands in the web. For the electorate to free itself from this interlocking directorate of the elites, the activist citizen must try to loosen if not sever each strand of the web one by one until more fairness and justice can be returned to the American democracy.

Thus, the powerlessness of the average citizen can also be rectified by a sweeping change in the income tax. Throw out the present code with its built-in loopholes and tax shelter payoffs to the few. As critics have said, this terrible monkey on the citizen's back has been designed to make the already rich richer and the poor poorer. Further, it's a citizen-paid subsidy to lawyers and accountants who, by their own admission, garner an estimated 70% of their fees from trying to steer hapless taxpayers through the present Byzantine code. Replace it with a fair, flat tax structure that gives no deductions to anyone, except for donations to charity, education or community causes. There would be no tax at all on incomes below a certain level—$20,000 has been suggested—which would be a boon to the struggling bottom levels of society. And the eventual tax form would be so simple that it could be filled out on a postcard.

To correct the economic and military excesses of American empire-building, many policies have been advanced by responsible people. Regarding corporate power overseas, require trans-nationals and their host countries to enforce worker justice worldwide—fair wages, workplace and environmental conditions raised if not to U.S. standards, at least above the slave wages paid in most of the 3rd World—or be penalized by U.S. law. If host countries refuse to comply, then products made there will be denied permission to our markets.

Also, for U.S. corporations that are dis-employing so many of our citizens by shipping their jobs overseas, it is suggested that some legislated portion of their overseas profits be plowed back into the welfare, re-training and job infrastructure here at home. Currently, corporations pay about 16% of our income taxes. In a recent <u>Business Week</u> poll, 73% of Americans felt that corporations have too much power. When top management begins to feel popular resistance to that power, the customer public not buying it anymore or even boycotting its products, corporations will be the first to make long-overdue changes in their policies, putting human values back into the equation, not just profits.

To stop the business wars that are perpetrating so much violence world-wide, qualified foreign policy specialists suggest: Outlaw by law any foreign military adventure where the armed forces of the U.S. are used to destabilize, terrorize or attack smaller nations when the sole reason is to protect U.S. corporate assets abroad, or to profit corporations with subsidies from those wars, paid by the taxpayer.

Germany, England, Japan, France and Italy all have well-known transnational corporations, doing business worldwide. But they see no need to support them by massive armies, fleets and a skein of military bases stretching across the globe. Why is it that only the U.S. feels it has to muscle in militarily? Could the answer be that the arms industry is the world's biggest business, and that the U.S. has the lion's share of it, to help fuel exactly the military-industrial complex that Eisenhower warned about. It's been suggested that the U.S. follow the peaceful model of foreign trade, encouraging friendship and cooperation with all nations, but outlawing political and business meddling in the affairs of any nation.

In that light, experts for years have been saying: abolish the CIA. It's a Cold War construct that grew out of the dirty tricks business of the old OSS. Though that organization did some heroic work in World War II, when it expanded into the giant bureaucracy of CIA, it lost most of its effectiveness. As a former CIA agent said, "I cannot point to one Agency operation, whether destabilization, assassination or outright proxy war where the CIA has succeeded in doing anything constructive for the American people."

In addition, there is no congressional oversight on how the CIA spends its money. In Vietnam, Iran-Contra and the Noriega affair, the CIA is known to have dirtied its hands in the international drug trade, and when any of its secret agents were exposed by the DEA, the Agency stepped in and halted prosecution. The offenders, it said, were its "assets." On the grounds of "national security" they couldn't be touched. CIA's entire mission has been cloaked in secrecy. If its role in defending the U.S. had been carried out efficiently, there's even the possibility that the nation might well have avoided the tragedy of September 11th.

Recommendations now on the table: disband **CIA,** "capitalism's invisible army," and merge its key personnel and technology into the intelligence structures of our present armed forces. **Failing such a drastic move, then the mission of CIA has to be rethought and revised, de-bureaucratized, and returned to its original mission which was to gather intelligence in foreign nations,** rather than attacking and destabilizing them.

As a further step, to lessen the impact of the U.S. economic/military empire that causes us to be hated as occupying conquerors in many nations, bring home all U.S. military from overseas bases. The question is asked: What are we doing with these people out there? Will an armored division in Germany stop an attack on us? And who will the attacker be? Russia is no longer a threat. In the event that we were militarily attacked anywhere in the world, our aircraft carriers and instant response forces can be rushed in overnight from the continental United States, exactly as they just have been in our attack on Afghanistan.

Further suggestions have been made that if and when we do remove our overseas American Empire bases, our

military units will not only be used to defend the continental U.S., but could well be a training force in the rebuilding of our infrastructure at home. Responsible economists have long proposed that our country needs a massive face-lift, much as the old Civilian Conservation Corps did during the Depression, not only employing the unemployed and teaching new skills, but upgrading the country as a more workable and pleasant place to live.

Few people remember that in the early 1920's, a young Army colonel, fed up with the service and wanting to retire, was given the unenviable job of driving a fleet of Army cars across the primitive road system of the U.S. It was a disaster. Many of the roads were no more than mud or gravel tracks. But the young colonel stuck with it. He was Dwight Eisenhower, and his recommendations led to the creation of our interstate highway system, the finest in the world.

None of this can be afforded, however, until U.S. Empire militarism stops sucking away $400 plus billion of the national budget. As one example of the bloated foreign policy establishment, does the public have any idea how many State Department people staff the U.S.

embassy in Paris? France is not one of our most vital trading partners nor are we at war in that area. But we have 1000 people in our Paris embassy. What do they do for the average citizen? Tour guides to show our visiting elites the best shops and restaurants? When President and Mrs. Clinton visited the embassy during their final term, they traveled with a staff of 600, flown in from the States, including personal hairdressers.

The final change that the citizen activist must work for is a return to the people of our civil liberties. In the wake of the tragedy in New York, in public response to government-media-induced fear, Americans are allowing their citizens' rights to be stripped away. It always happens in war, Lincoln jailing thousands during the Civil War, suspending the rights of the press as well. The same happened in the imprisonment of German-Americans during World War I, and the gross injustice of interning Japanese Americans in World War II.

Americans don't want to live in a police state, trading their freedoms for some illusory "safety" that can never be. Many jurists are suggesting decentralizing power from the federal down to the local levels. End repressive federal police power and the illegal wire-taps and harassment that go with it.

End also the other major extension of the war mentality, the war against drugs. In the 1970's, the U.S. had 2 federal agencies fighting drugs, on a budget of $11 million a year. Now the U.S. has 21 federal agencies plus all the armed services on a budget of $19 billion a year— and more drugs are in the country than ever before. The nation incarcerates 2 million Americans, a city the size of Dallas, the largest prison population in the world. Of that number, 1 million of those convicts, a city the size of Ft. Worth, are in jail for their victimless crimes of being connected to drugs in some way.

Drugs have been a federally-created Enemy Out There, one more demon with which to control the citizenry. The failed experiment of Prohibition in the '20's and 30's created a mafia at home. Present Drug Prohibition has created a worldwide mafia whose $400 billion yearly income is larger than that of the entire automobile industry and pays not a cent in taxes. A few courageous politicians like the governor of New Mexico and authors as diverse in the political spectrum as Gore

Vidal, William Buckley, Harpers magazine and economist Milton Friedman have been saying for years: Repeal the failed drug laws. Take the crime out of it as FDR did by ending alcohol prohibition. Let the states decide whether they'll be wet or dry, and let them enforce it themselves.

Because of decades of drug war propaganda, many Americans have been led to believe that the problem is distasteful at best and probably insoluble. What U.S. media has failed to report, however, is that the European Union is fast moving way from the draconian punishments practiced by the U.S. Says Paul Flynn, an English Labor Party MP: "The drug war, in Europe at least, is essentially over." The British Home secretary announced in October that his government would stop arresting people for marijuana use "or even cautioning them," as well as expanding legal distribution of heroin to addicts. In the mid-'70's, the Dutch were the first Europeans to back away from the U.S.-led drug war with positive results. "After 25 years of intelligent, pragmatic policies, drugs in the Netherlands seem to cause the least harm to individuals and society." MP Flynn is a member of the Health Commission for the Council of Europe which recommends policies to its 41 member nations.

The miracle of rising consciousness is that many of the solutions are already evident. In millions of minds unknown to each other, gifted visionaries or ordinary citizens have already glimpsed what needs to be done. They don't need experts to give them a road map. We need common sense.

Recently in Tucson, Arizona—not necessarily a hotbed of activism—thousands of citizens were so moved by September 11th that they joined together and took out full page newspaper ads. They put their names and their money on the line to protest what they felt was our rushing to war in Afghanistan. They opposed the massive, militaristic war propaganda, the bombings and inevitable civilian deaths, to say nothing of the hatred our violence is causing in other Muslim nations. Instead, they recommended that we treat the New York attack as a crime against humanity, and that with combined intelligence and police work, we, other nations and the

UN, pursue the criminals and bring them to legal justice in our own courts and the World Court.

If such responsible protest can happen in Tucson, it seems only a matter of time before similar citizens groups will make their voices heard all across the land. Certainly, as in Tucson, they'll receive the scorn and catcalls. Talk radio shows will be jammed with other "patriots" calling the protestors "traitors," undermining the holy war of our country. Here again, it's like the Vietnam war. Ordinary people and particularly politicians were afraid to stand up against it, fearing that they'd be labeled "soft on communism." But when the public had finally found it's "strong loud voice unafraid," as William Faulkner said, the ill-advised war was ended before it tore the nation apart, and the troops were brought home.

For all the horror of September 11th, for all TV's mything and dumbing, its positive value could be that it's helping to make all of us into one. It's hard not to mourn Afghan Taliban women weeping over the mistaken deaths of their children from a misguided American missile. The same for our friendly-fired dead

Marines. It's hard not to shiver in compassion at the blackened bodies on the Iraq desert, or the hundreds of thousands of children the U.S. embargo has killed there for lack of food or medicine. A government can't run wars when the public sees the faces in them, the Enemy's and our own. The nation learned it in Vietnam. In those black body bags are us. We're beyond circling the wagons or charging up San Juan Hill with our flag— beyond because our rising consciousness tells us that we've outgrown the conviction that we white Americans living on a modest portion of the earth are God's only chosen people, and all the rest just do not count.

How to help end violence?

Reason is the road to truth. Centuries ago, the great philosopher Socrates taught that the "golden cord of reason" is what allows mankind to resist the whims and caprice of dark forces like violence. He warned that if we lose that reason, suspend criticality, accept anything that custom serves up, then you and I become puppets on a string, and the form of life we are living is the life of a slave.

Just such reason fuels the words of Lewis Lapham, editor of <u>Harpers magazine</u>. He writes that war propaganda following September 11th served the purposes of "Washington's political and intelligence establishments anxious to shore up their authority in the aftermath of a calamity that revealed the magnitude of their stupidity and incompetence.

"The attack was an attack on American foreign policy which, for the last thirty years has allied itself both at home and abroad with despotism and the weapons trade, a policy conducted by and for a relatively small cadre of selfish interests, unrepresentative of (and unaccountable to) the American people as a whole.

"I give the American people a higher quotient of intelligence and a greater store of idealism than their supervisors in Washington think they want or deserve, and I suspect that if given a voice in the nation's foreign affairs they would endorse the policies (similar to those once put forward by Franklin D. Roosevelt) that reflected a concern for human rights, international law, nuclear disarmament, freedom from both the colonial and neocolonial economic monopoly.

"But the American people don't have a voice at the table, especially not now, not during what the media and the government aggressively promote as 'a time of war.'"

"Our world," wrote British pacifist Bertrand Russell, "has sprouted a weird concept of security and a warped sense of morality. Weapons are sheltered like treasures and children are exposed to incineration."

Says Richard Rohr, the renowned Franciscan priest and prophet: "Just as the Taliban can corrupt Mohammed, so have we been able to corrupt and use Jesus for our own cultural needs. How then do we become light and hope against such archetypal and irrational forms of evil? First, we must deny terrorists their victory by refusing to mirror them and do the same thing in reactionary and disguised form. This is the only true moral victory. We must not transmit and continue our human pain but must somehow transform it into a new kind of humanity, a new mind, a different society.

"We must find a new consciousness. We must make sure that our light is not just disguised forms of vengeance, fear, political expediency or knee-jerk political reaction. And by that I mean both knee-jerk pacifism as much as knee-jerk patriotism. **Neither of them are 'from God.'**

"Jesus' plan for social transformation is to free people from the system and thus unlock it inevitably from the inside. I believe it is just such people who have always kept humanity and institutions from a history of total violence. They are indeed the light of the world without even knowing it.

"As God said to Abraham, 'For the sake of ten just people, I will spare the whole city.' All it takes is for a small minority to stop believing the lie and the lie will die. All it takes is for a committed minority to believe in Love, and Love will use them as a channel into the whole world."

*

I wonder now if it wasn't love that led me at last beyond war and to a place called Paradise Island.

In 1973, after weeks of traveling around the Pacific, revisiting my old battlegrounds of Guam and Pelelieu, I was not only drained by the heat which had never bothered me at 22, but more than this, the rust, junk and death still staining all the islands seemed so forgotten, so meaningless. I just wanted to get the hell home and forget it. But Teddy said, No, we'd come this far, we had to take it through to the end, which was our last scheduled stop, Truk atoll.

It was not a memory that I wanted to re-live.

Far out in the Caroline Islands, Truk had been the main Japanese fortress in the Pacific. It was their Pearl Harbor from which their fleets and aircraft had been attacking us throughout the war. Truk's giant scatter of islands were so impregnable that all of us dreaded going anywhere near them.

Unfortunately, we didn't have a choice. After General Geiger had declared Guam secured, we flew him back to his headquarters on Guadalcanal. To keep him out of harm's way, we'd had to give Truk a wide berth, flying instead via the safe Marshall island of Eniwetok and then south to the Solomons. It was a grueling 17 hour trip. We were all pretty jumpy and worn out. For two weeks during the Guam battle, we'd been living under the wing of our plane, being treated nightly to sniper fire, and in one case, to a Japanese soldier who must have stepped right over us, but mercifully left us alone. His target was a Corsair fighter parked next to us. He crawled in behind the armor seat and when the Marine pilot got into the cockpit for a dawn flight, the Japanese blew up the plane and himself with two grenades. The pilot wasn't even scratched. The Japanese hadn't figured on the armor seat.

We'd no sooner landed Geiger safely on Guadalcanal when he came up into the cockpit and told us that we'd have to turn around as soon as we were gassed up, and fly back to Guam that same night. But this night, which was August 13, 1944, we wouldn't have the luxury of taking the long way around. Instead, he was sending us directly through the lethal Truk airspace.

The urgency, we were later told, was to bring back to Geiger crates of plans for the Pelelieu operation, less than a month away. His staff officers had been working on them during the Guam operation.

To make the trip by this quickest route, we'd have to fly a thousand miles north from a U.S. held island,

Emirau. The idea was to sneak past Truk the first night, and if we made it, turn around and tip-toe back the same route the next night. We'd have to do it alone, no escort. Fighters didn't have the range to accompany us. The Navy commander at Emirau had just had a patrol bomber shot down in the same vicinity. He tried to cancel our flight but Geiger countermanded him. Send them, the General said, and we went. Our only armament was two Thompson submachine guns.

To pull it off, we'd have to hit in the darkness a 60 mile slot between two atolls, Puluwat and Lamotrek, less than a hundred miles from the main Truk atoll. One had an enemy fighter strip, the other a seaplane base. Should we drift too close to either one, their radar would pick us up and they'd blow us out of the sky.

We were lucky the first night. The stars were out. Using celestial navigation, we strained our eyes for any speck of island below us, but saw only the blackness of the sea. We must have hit the slot. Landing in the dawn at Guam, we slept all day in a wrecked building. By dusk, somebody rousted us out. We went down to Orote strip and loaded aboard the crates of plans for Pelelieu that the staff officers were working on.

Then came a moment of truth. Standing beside our faithful, coral-caked R4D (the old DC-3 of the airlines) which at the blinding speed of 140 knots had so long carried us safely through all Geiger's battlegrounds—we stood and stared up at the sky. Rain was already stinging our faces. No problem, we'd had a year and a half so far of fighting angry Pacific weather. But nothing like the cyclonic wind that was hitting us now and tearing off our baseball caps. One of the blackest, lightning-flashed storms we'd ever seen was roaring down on Guam. A bitch, almost hurricane strength. There was no way around it. We'd have to sock right into it to get home.

We'd barely roared up off of Orote strip before the rain began lacing us as if some giant were flinging buckets of gravel into our face. Blinding waves of rain were so powerful that they hammered through the frayed rubber window seals and soaked us in the cockpit. The turbulence was violent. We'd pop down landing gear and flaps, cut throttle trying to slow the roller coaster, but massive thunderheads were flinging us two thousand feet a minute upward at 95 knots. We'd tremble there a moment, pick up flaps and gear, shove throttles to the firewall. No use. The next thunderhead would slam us roaring back down, two thousand feet a minute, engines screaming at 195 knots which was far more than the plane should stand.

We were wildly out of control. No visible sky above, no sea below. We had no stars to shoot, no drift sights, nothing to steer by. It was impossible to hit our slot between Puluwat and Lamotrek. It was strictly dead reckoning now, and if we reckoned wrong, dead we'd likely be.

When we neared the estimated position of Puluwat and Lamotrek, we shut off our radios. We literally tried to whisper past whatever was below us. When the radioman spotted running lights paralleling us, he shouted: "Jap!" It must have been. We think a Betty bomber, heavily armed and possibly looking for us in the wildness of the storm.

The only thing we could do was to plunge into massive, fisting thunderheads and lose ourselves. The Pacific at night is such an enormous blackness that when you're lost within it, you almost want to weep at the futility of ever hoping to survive such violence. And we had five hours of it still to go.

We'd zigged and zagged so much that finally we had no idea where the tiny speck of Emirau island lay. Our one hope by then was to pick up either the radio range or the homing beacon that had been recently installed on the island. But these were still primitive instruments, reaching only a hundred miles or so. The static of the storm was also garbling the signals. We tried the radio range and its signal never seemed to get louder. Then we switched to the homer with the same result. In the darkness of the cockpit we stared at each other. What the hell was going on? On the radio compass dial, the range and the homer were giving us positions sixty degrees apart. How could this be when the island was so small that the two towers had to be less than a mile apart.

We had to choose. Which was the true signal?

For some reason, we chose the homer and began roaring down its dark path in the sky. Several moments later, the radioman thrust into the cockpit. Good kid, he wouldn't give up. He was clenching a frequency book.

Townsville, Australia, he cried, had the same frequency as the homer on Emirau. Could it be that in the violence of the storm, Townsville's stronger signal was hitting the ionosphere and bouncing back to us? If that were the case, at 8,000 feet, we were minutes away from slamming into the 12,000 foot Owen Stanley Range in New Guinea.

We made a screaming turn off of the homer and back onto the weaker range. The signal didn't grow or give any hope that we were closing on the island. It was procedure to use a new code book for every day, the radioman tapping out puzzles in Morse that the enemy couldn't break. But we were way past that now. Navy regs went out the window. In forbidden plain English, we begged Emirau tower that if they heard us, turn a searchlight up at the sky.

I don't know how long it took then, still banging around in rain and fisted by thunderheads. In gritted silence, staring at our faces in the cockpit windshield, one of us cried out. A distant flash of light in the dark clouds. We broke into a cheer, roaring down a few minutes later onto the rain-soaked Emirau runway. Our gas gauge needles were ticking on empty.

Well, we'd made it, beat the sky. And the rest of the trip would be a lark. We only had five hours left to Guadalcanal, but we'd be flying now down across the conquered islands, the Solomons Slot, an American lake, safe as a church. We gassed up and at about 2 a.m. took off again.

We hadn't even reached cruising altitude when the radioman rushed up to the cockpit. Our IFF—identification friend or foe signal—had just burned out. Meaning that for the next five hours, we'd be showing up on radar as a Japanese bogey. On all the various islands we'd be passing, eager U.S. night fighters would be scrambling, howling up, homed into us by radar—couldn't see our stars in the dark. Just lock on—boom!

We sent the radioman back to get on his key, and one by one rattle out to every squadron that we were friendly, leave us the hell alone, and pray. We fled through the long darkness with our shoulders hunched up, waiting for the flash that never came. Somebody had us by the hand. The first real light we saw were streaks of dawn, over the jungles of Guadalcanal. Somebody said, "That lovely sonofabitch," and we went on in to land.

So why was it, I wonder, that now, nearly 30 years later, I'd be in a Pacific rain squall again, down on the coral of that once-fearsome island, Truk. Though I was already soaked, I happened to run down the beach and take shelter under the palm fronds of a fisherman's shack. Beside me was the fisherman himself, a brown-skinned Trukese native in a breechclout. He was trying to light his limp home-made cigarette. Fortunately, I had the kind of Zippo we used in the war. It still worked enough to get him fired up.

We stood there like wet puppies, grinning in a kind of smoker's pidgin English. On the wet brown skin of his back, I noticed ugly scars, great long welts. How come? I asked. "Japan time," he said. They had bayonetted him and forced him to work for them building airfields. He sucked at the cigarette and his coffee eyes studied me. "You know Japan time? You come here like other 'Merican guys, break oil tanks, plenty smoke, bomb going off?"

I said no, that was the big carrier strike in '44, but a few months later, I did fly near here for a couple of nights, through Puluwat and Lamotrek.

He howled. "Lamotrek!" He clasped my hand, then threw his arms around me. "I raised on Lamotrek! Home island. Maybe I there them nights! Look up in sky, see you!"

With the rain drumming the thatch roof, we talked long of the wartime days until finally he gripped both of my hands. "Yah, we same, you know us here, we friends. Hey, 'Merican guy, I got place you gonna see. Beautiful. Best we got. Tomorrow, I take you in my fishing boat. What you think? We go Paradise Island!"

Oh, come on, I thought. Was this a tourist scam or something he was making up?

But Paradise existed and we went to it the next day. Max, the fisherman, his boat boy David, Teddy and me. At the last minute, while we were loading our gear into Max's boat, a shy young Japanese approached us. He did the requisite bows, and not wanting to interfere, but might we take him with us on our trip?

Max scowled and said something in Japanese that must have been nasty. The young man flinched but still smiled. Max shrugged then, life is like that in the islands. Accept. So we had a passenger from Tokyo. Akio was his name, a sweet, earnest young employee of the Japanese Tourist Bureau. Down here to explore tourist facilities in the area, he was prototype Japanese, white shorts and shirt, knee socks and camera around his neck. He kept thanking us effusively for including him.

But as we roared across Truk lagoon, the largest in the world, I think Akio began to regret coming along. Max was running the tiller of his outboard with his bare foot, and even over the noise of his Johnson 50 horse, he was barking angry Japanese at Akio. They were re-fighting their war now, obviously the abuses Max had suffered as a prisoner. Akio would turn away, his face so tight with humiliation that Teddy and I felt embarrassed to watch. But then, like an island storm, it swept on past. Max scrambled up to the bow and flung out his arm. "There, 'Merican guy! Paradise!"

It was spectacular, a fragment of island no more than a reef, white sand beaches shaded with palms. Inland, beyond a thicket of heavy mangroves, I could make out the seaward side, naked battlements of coral, pounded by the open Pacific and thundering misty spume hundreds of feet into the air. The roar was constant and awesome, a symphony of rainbows, seabirds arching in screaming parabolas and plunging into the shattering waves for prey.

Max slowed the boat and we glided over vermilion and ochre coral gardens. Schools of brightly colored fish drifted below us through forests of yellow lace. They didn't seem to sense our presence. They made no attempt to run away. When Teddy and I slid into the warm softness of the water and coasted through the coral gardens in the suck and hiss of our snorkels, the fish were so tame they'd stream between our legs. Some would even gup their mouths on the strange taste of our tennis shoes.

"Bad sharks here?" I asked David, our boat boy who was paddling beside us. He was grinning, wearing a mar-mar headband of green leaves. "No bad." A moment later, a dark shadow appeared in my face mask. An eight foot shark, lazily studying us and drifting on past.

The scene was so fierce and primeaval, so remote from any "civilized" world that I seemed to lose consciousness of time and my place within it. Here, I was part of the eternal struggle of the coral to replenish itself. I was the crash and suck and refueling of the waves, my energy somehow tied to all of it. The trembling reef beneath my feet was connected in its bedrock to the ancient burned-out volcanoes that had formed the atolls of Puluwat and Lamotrek. My nights of fear above those islands—how insignificant they'd been against nature's flaming struggles through her eons of time. That was the real and only war, the nobility of her life force, pulsing in every particle of living matter, coding into them the ultimate meaning that life would prevail.

Behind me I heard a human cry, and reluctantly I turned away from the thundering reef. Akio was dog-paddling toward me, spluttering apologies. I'd loaned him my spin-fishing rod, and now he'd managed to lose my only lure. He was determined to send me a dozen lures from Japan, please?

I smiled and told him to forget it. We hadn't really come here to fish. But as we paddled on together into a hidden bay, I spotted something that wrenched me back to the past, and old wars gone down.

A silver metal fin was protruding from the shallow water. I gulped a deep breath and dove, then blew out a gasp of astonishment. Resting on the soft sand bottom was a Zero fighter, not a mark of rust on it or a scar. It appeared to have landed here moments before. I clung to the canopy of the open cockpit, fully expecting to see a skeleton within. But there was only emptiness and the red needle of the airspeed indicator ticking in tiny bubbles.

Akio clung to the tail section as I made repeated dives. In the sand I found a fragment of the Zero's wing flap, which seemed to be the only damage when the pilot crash-landed. As I carried the relic back to shore, my mind was spinning. Who was in that plane? Had he been some eager, untried youth, fighting our fleet in the carrier strike? Did he parachute out? Or could it have been possible that he, too, had been ordered to fly that night of August 14, sent up into the storm to chase an American bogey that had somehow slipped away between Puluwat and Lamotrek?

Lost in the enigma of it, I sat in the warm sand and studied the fragment of the wing flap. Akio knelt beside me. I showed him splinters of wood, laminated between the Zero's outer skin. I was amazed that they'd used wood. Akio nodded. Yes, bamboo. That's all Japan had left by the end of the war.

His voice had tightened, his eyelids squeezed shut. In dignity, he was weeping. At first I pretended not to notice, but then he touched my arm gently and said, "It is Japan's fault, all this here. Fighting war. So much destruction, so much horror we caused. I knew nothing about it. I wasn't born then. But my father had to go. He fought..." He shook his head and tears ran down his cheeks. "What we did, I am so sorry..."

When I answered, my throat was tight. "It's nobody's fault," I said. "Put it behind us. It's done now."

Then, in a moment, the awkwardness was gone. From down the beach Max was shouting to us. He'd speared a giant clam and came sloshing in from the reef with a purpling, blobby object in his hand. By the time Akio and I reached him, he'd sliced the muscle from the clam and was drenching it in lime juice and soy sauce. We ate it raw, washing it down with Kirin beer, and then stretched out under the palm trees.

Teddy lay sunburned in the sand and looked as lithe as she had at 21. Even the sea tousle of my hair I could consider as resembling salt, not grey. Whatever our delusions, we felt a youth and liberation, unfettered by wrist watches and the baggage of our cares. Trukese, Japanese, American, we seemed joined into the life force, our strangeness to each other and our enmities fading away.

As if to heighten the unreality, we began hearing new sounds from out on the reef. Distant dots moved toward us across the coral flats until they became native canoes. Tapping their paddles against the wooden hulls, two boatloads of Trukese fishermen glided up to our beach. Max hailed them and they spilled out, the women waddling up in their bright mumus, several of them squatting shamelessly in the shallows to complete their toilets before joining us. Max told me that these were several families of fishermen, from babes at the breast to wizened elders with blue tattoos in the wrinkles of their cheeks. They lay with us in the shade of the mangroves, their brown limbs melting into the sand in instant relaxation.

Time and ambition seemed meaningless to them. They were children of the Stone Age, and how they could laugh! A young girl lazily draped her arm around me. That was funny. Then, she tweaked my beaky nose— that was hilarious. The others were belching, rumbling, snoring, and when they drifted back to wakefulness, their eyes caught the endless reflection of the sea. Soon, with Max translating, they began telling us tales of the great ocean voyages of the Micronesian people. They spoke of the Magic Men who were trained generation after generation to guide the canoes across thousands of miles of open sea. Riding with them, too, were the Navigator Men who could track the stars with the naked eye, watch the direction of birds and the coloration of the water to give them their bearings.

Sea life, they called it, and to preserve their lives on their journeys was the Shark Man. Trained from childhood to sing a special mantra, he could slip into the water and confront a massive shark that was threatening the canoe. Because ocean waves swamped the canoes, these Micronesians were often sitting in water with the shark's great fin only a few feet away. But armed only with his mantra chant, the Shark Man would approach the monster, gentle him until he could rub his belly. Then he'd slip a mar mar of palm leaves over the shark's head and he'd drift harmlessly away.

I glanced at Teddy. She was sitting bolt upright, half-frown, half rapture. Could we believe such a thing? No, certainly not back home in our normal lives. But Paradise Island, the sudden confronting of the past buried within us, the primeaval spirit—was this not also home, the real one?

Then, like most moments of grace, too soon it was over. Without any predetermined signal, the Trukese left us, their laughter trailing down to their canoes, and their footprints in the sand were slowly washed away by the creeping tide.

They disappeared toward the falling sun until they were tiny specks again, floating off to probe some other reef. We, too, departed then, our bodies sunburned, our limbs soft and nerveless from hours in the sea. As we rumbled across the enormity of Truk atoll, a night of yellowish stars closed over us. Sometime in the long trip home, Akio, perhaps thinking of his own wife, said to

Teddy: "Ah, madam, please tell me: what flowers do you choose for your arrangements?"

I stared at him in the darkness. You, my enemy? You the demon I was taught to hate? How many more must there be before we go beyond? Something in me died here, and was being re-born.

Then the enormity of stars closed over us. In the rising of the moon, the Southern Cross was still as bright as it was that night it navigated us through those islands. Teddy smiled at Akio and told him the flowers she likes in her arrangements. Together, with only the boat's silver wake to remind us of how far we'd come, we rumbled on again toward home.

*

Maybe the Good Book says it best:
Our Father who art in heaven—
Forgive us our trespasses as we forgive those who trespass against us
Lead us not into temptation
But deliver us from evil—

The kingdom, the power and the glory.

Someday.

Otis Carney

ABOUT THE AUTHOR

Otis Carney is the author of seventeen books, including the best sellers *When the Bough Breaks* and *New Lease on Life*. In film and TV, he has created series and screenplays for major studios and networks, for such actors as Jack Webb of *Dragnet,* Marlon Brando, and John Wayne. The winner of Freedom Foundation and Western Heritage awards, he does occasional journalism and has written for presidential candidates.

According to the *New York Times,* his landmark campaign film *Choice* was "unique...a forerunner that enduringly altered political discourse in the U.S."

A graduate of Princeton and a Marine Corps captain, he flew for twenty-two months in the Pacific during World War II. Mr. Carney and Teddy, his wife of fifty-five years, have three sons, seven grandchildren and are cattle ranchers in Wyoming and Arizona.

Printed in the United States
931900003B